COTTAGE

COOKING

COOKING

Chef
Ted Reader

W

Warwick Publishing

Toronto   Los Angeles

Front cover: Grilled Greek Salad, page 43

ISBN: 1-895629-76-4

Published by:
Warwick Publishing Inc., 388 King Street West, Toronto, Ontario M5V 1K2
Warwick Publishing Inc., 1424 N. Highland Avenue, Los Angeles, CA 90027

Distributed by:
Firefly Books Ltd., 3680 Victoria Park Avenue, Willowdale, Ontario M2H 3K1

Design: Diane Farenick
Editorial Services: Melinda Tate
Food Consultant: Charles Cole
Photographs: Heather Halfyard
Kitchen Accessories and Dishes courtesy of DETAILS - DETAILS, St. Catharines, Ontario

Printed and bound in Canada

CONTENTS

Introduction

Barbecuing is a wonderful way of enjoying food in the summertime. It's very relaxing. Instead of heating up the cottage kitchen, you're blending the fresh outdoor air with the delicious aroma of grilled food.

Barbecuing is also social and casual. People say all good parties end up in the kitchen; when you cook on the barbecue, you'll notice people tend to gather around. Everyone wants to be a part of the barbecue, everyone wants to see what's going on, and everyone likes to make fun of the barbecue chef. Barbecue is the art of the fire. The heat, the smoke, and the whole social aspect create magic.

Barbecuing sears in the juices. The flavors of the smoke, the charcoal chari-ness on the outside of the food, the almost-burning singe—all heighten your palate so that you really crave it. Whatever you cook on, from a small hibachi or bowl barbecue to a gas or electric grill, you're taken back to an era before kitchens and your instinctive love of food cooked on a fire. Once you're hooked, you will want to grill everything.

And you can grill anything...eggs....creme brulé... any kind of seafood...veg-etables... even bread. With a few modifications, anything can be cooked on a barbecue as easily as in an indoor oven or on a stove.

People tend to stick to the old barbecue standards like steak and burgers but they shouldn't be afraid to experiment. I hope *Cottage Cooking* will show that grilling can be both fun and versatile.

SOUPS

CHARRED TOMATO SOUP

THE CHARRING IS WHAT GIVES THIS SOUP ITS MEXICAN/SOUTHWESTERN FLAVOR.

THIS SOUP IS GREAT FOR LUNCH OR DINNER, AND IS TASTY COLD.

8	large field tomatoes
6	plum tomatoes
1 large	spanish onion, peeled and sliced
1	red chili pepper
1 head	elephant garlic, peeled
1 tbsp	extra virgin olive oil
4 1/2 cups	chicken or vegetable stock
2 tbsp	fresh coriander
1 cup	corn kernels (fresh or frozen)
	salt and pepper to taste
1	avocado, peeled and diced 1/2"
8	flour tortillas, grilled

1. On a pre-heated grill over medium heat, char the tomatoes, onion, chili and garlic for 10-15 minutes.

2. Once the vegetables have been charred (they should be speckled with black char, but not too burnt), place them in a medium-sized pot.

3. Add the olive oil and sauté for 2 minutes over high heat, stirring constantly.

4. Add the chicken stock and the fresh coriander. Bring to a boil and turn heat to low. Let simmer for 45-60 minutes, until all of the flavors have blended together.

5. Place soup in a blender (or use a hand mixer) and purée until smooth.

6. Return to the pot and return to boil over medium heat. Add the corn and simmer for 10 minutes longer to fully cook the corn.

7. Season with salt and pepper and serve. Garnish with diced avocado and grilled flour tortillas.

SERVES 6 TO 8.

CORN CHOWDER

═══════════

IF YOU HAVE ANY LEFTOVER CORN ON THE COB, CHAR THEM UP AND PUT THEM

INTO THIS SOUP. MY FAVORITE CORN IS SILVER QUEEN, FROM MARYLAND.

PEACHES AND CREAM CORN IS DELICIOUS.

THIS IS THE PERFECT SOUP FOR A COOL EVENING IN LATE SUMMER.

═══════════

3 tbsp	butter
1	medium-sized onion, diced
2 cloves	garlic, finely chopped
1 cup	white of leeks, coarsely chopped
3 cups	medium-sized potatoes, diced
3 cups	grilled corn *
4 cups	chicken or vegetable stock
1/2 cup	heavy cream
to taste	salt and pepper

1. In a large soup pot melt butter over medium heat, stir in and cook the onions, garlic, leeks and potatoes for approximately 5 to 7 minutes.

2. Add the stock, allow to simmer for 10 minutes.

3. To finish off add the grilled corn and cream.

4. Remove from heat and season with salt and pepper.

5. Serve with Tuscan Bread Salad (page 45), roasted peppers and cherry tomatoes.

*Soak corn in cold water with husks and silk intact for 1 hour. Place on the barbecue over medium-high heat and cook for 20 minutes, turning them every 5 minutes. Let corn cool, remove husk and then using a sharp knife, cut kernels from the cob.

SERVES 6.

GRILLED WILD MUSHROOM SOUP

A PORTOBELLO MUSHROOM IS BETTER THAN EATING A STEAK, IT'S SO RICH.

I WOULD SERVE THIS SOUP WITH GRILLED BREAD, RUSTIC OR SOURDOUGH,

AND A PINOT NOIR OR CABERNET SAUVIGNON.

2 cups	crimini brown mushrooms, halved
2 cups	oyster mushrooms, halved
2 cups	shiitake mushrooms, quartered and stems removed
1 cup	chanterelle mushrooms
2 cups	sliced portobello mushrooms
1 cup	sliced red onion, 1/4 inch thick
1/4 cup	chopped fresh shallots
2 tbsp	chopped fresh thyme
2 tbsp	olive oil
2 tbsp	chopped garlic
1/4 cup	Bourbon whisky
4 cups	chicken or vegetable stock
1/8 cup	balsamic vinegar
	salt and pepper to taste

1. Wipe mushrooms with a damp cloth. Remove stems and reserve for other use.

2. Place mushrooms and red onion in a barbecue basket and grill over medium-high heat for 6 minutes per side, until the mushrooms are tender and slightly charred.

3. While the mushrooms are cooking, sauté the garlic, shallots, and thyme in the olive oil, in a large pot over medium-high heat, for 2 minutes until tender.

4. Add the grilled mushrooms, red onion, and continue to sauté for 2 minutes. Add the bourbon, chicken stock, vinegar, and salt and pepper to taste.

5. Bring to a boil and reduce heat to medium low. Let simmer for 10 minutes.

SERVES 4 TO 6.

SEAFOOD BOUILLABAISE

A CLASSIC FRENCH DISH THAT I'VE ADAPTED FOR THE BARBECUE.

THIS COULD BE A MEAL ON ITS OWN.

Broth:

1 cup	pressed or crushed tomatoes
16-20	saffron stamens
2 cups	fish stock

Fish and Seafood:

12	bacon-wrapped scallops
4 large	jumbo shrimp
6 oz	salmon fillet
4 oz	tuna steak
4 oz	swordfish steak
4 oz	cod fillet
3 large	lobster tails (in the shell, scored down the back)
3/4 cup	olive oil
	cracked black pepper

1. Combine broth ingredients in a saucepan and bring to a simmer; simmer for 10-15 minutes.

2. Remove saffron with a strainer or leave in for color. Keep warm.

3. Coat all the seafood with olive oil and pepper.

4. Grill all the seafood for approximately 10-12 minutes.

5. Cut seafood into soupspoon-sized pieces. Place in a tureen.

6. Ladle broth over top of seafood.

7. Divide among 4-6 soup plates. Serve with grilled flatbread and olive oil.

SERVES 4 TO 6.

APPETIZERS

SUMMER DIPS

SUMMER DIPS ADD A BIT OF FRESHNESS TO THE SUMMER. THEY'RE A GREAT WAY TO START A PARTY. YOU'RE SKINNY DIPPING IN THE LAKE, YOU WANT TO BE DIPPING WHEN YOU EAT. BUT NO DOUBLE DIPPING! SERVE THESE DIPS WITH THE GRILLED BREADS, PITAS, OR VEGGIES.

BABBA GANOOSH

6	eggplants
3	large Spanish onions
4 tbsp	garlic chopped
2 tbsp	cumin
2 cups	mayonnaise
1 tsp	Louisiana hot sauce
1/2 cup	lemon juice
1/2 cup	olive oil
	salt and pepper to taste

1. Peel, salt and rinse eggplants. Roast until soft.

2. In a food processor, blend all ingredients until smooth.

3. Chill for 1 to 2 hours.

4. Serve with pita bread or your favorite fresh bread.

BLUE CHEESE DIP

1 cup	mayonnaise
1 cup	sour cream
3 oz	blue cheese
2	medium jalapeño peppers, finely diced
1 tbsp	lemon juice
	salt and pepper to taste

1. In a large mixing bowl, blend mayonnaise, sour cream, blue cheese until smooth.

2. Add remaining ingredients, mix, season with salt and pepper to taste.

Serve with Tequila Wings.

GUACAMOLE

4	avocados, peeled and seeded
2 tbsp	lemon juice
1 tbsp	olive oil
1/4 cup	diced onion
1/2 cup	diced tomato
1 tsp	chopped garlic
	salt and pepper to taste
2 dashes	Louisiana hot sauce
1 tbsp	chopped fresh coriander

1. In a food processor, puree the avocados with the lemon juice and olive oil until smooth.

2. Remove from food processor and place in a large mixing bowl. Add remaining ingredients and season to taste.

3. Chill for 1 to 2 hours and serve with the fajitas, or as a dip.

MAKES 2 CUPS.

HUMMOS

GREAT WITH GRILLED FLAT BREADS AND PITA!

19 oz	can of chick peas, drained
1/2 cup	sour cream
2 tbsp	tahini
3 tbsp	olive oil
1 tbsp	lemon juice
	salt and pepper to taste
1/4 tsp	cayenne pepper
1/4 tbsp	cumin
1 tbsp	chopped parsley
2 tbsp	chopped fresh garlic

1. In a food processor, blend all ingredients together until smooth.

2. Chill for 1 to 2 hours.

SERVES 6 TO 8.

GARLIC BREAD

1 large	French stick or 2 baguettes
1 lb	salted butter
1/2 cup	chopped parsley, basil, oregano
1 1/2 tbsp	fresh chopped garlic
1/2 cup	grated swiss cheese
1/2 cup	grated cheddar cheese

1. Preheat grill to medium-high heat.

2. Cut the bread in half lengthwise.

3. Mix the butter, herbs and garlic together in a bowl. Spread mixture over each bread-half with a knife or rubber spatula.

4. Wrap bread in aluminum foil. Place on the grill, and heat for 10-15 minutes, turning once.

5. Remove bread from grill. Keep it in the foil until ready to serve.

SERVES 6 TO 8.

GREEK-STYLE BARBECUE PITA

3 tbsp	olive oil
2 tbsp	lemon juice
1 tbsp	chopped fresh oregano
1 tbsp	chopped garlic
	salt and freshly ground pepper to taste
12 to 16	Greek-style pitas

1. Mix the olive oil, lemon juice, oregano, garlic and salt and pepper. Set aside.

2. Over medium heat grill the pitas brushing both sides with the olive oil and garlic mixture.

3. Cook until the pitas are golden brown and crispy.

SERVES 6 TO 8.

GRILLED BREADS

20 slices of foccacia, baguettes, or pizza crusts
1/2 cup   balsamic vinegar
1/2 cup   roasted garlic olive oil
               softened goat cheese
               grated parmesan cheese

1. Whisk the olive oil and balsamic vinegar together in a bowl; season with salt and pepper, if desired.

2. Brush some of the mixture onto an assortment of breads.

3. Place bread directly onto a seasoned barbecue, brushed-side down. Cooking time will vary depending on size and thickness of bread.

4. Top some of the breads with goat cheese and/or parmesan. Close the lid of the barbecue to melt the cheese.

5. Finish the cheese-topped bread with a couple of twists of the pepper mill.

SERVES 8 TO 10.

BARBECUE FAJITAS

ARIBA, MAN! FAJITAS OUT OF THE FRYING PAN AND ONTO THE FIRE.

JUST IMAGINE THE FUN YOU'LL HAVE COOKING THESE UP FOR YOUR AMIGOS.

1/4 cup   soya sauce
1 tsp   sesame oil
1 tsp   Louisiana hot sauce
1 tsp   chili flakes
1 tsp   chopped oregano
4 tbsp   chopped garlic
1 lb   flank steak

1/4 cup	lime juice
4 tsp	freshly ground black pepper
1 tbsp	chopped coriander
1/4 cup	olive oil
4	4-oz boneless, skinless chicken breasts
1 cup	red pepper, julienned
1 cup	green pepper, julienned
1 cup	yellow pepper, julienned
1 cup	red onion, sliced
	salt and freshly ground black pepper to taste
12	flour tortillas

1. In a medium-sized dish, combine the soya sauce, sesame oil, hot sauce, chili flakes, oregano, and 1 tbsp of chopped garlic. Marinate the flank steak in this mixture for 6 to 8 hours or overnight in the refrigerator.

2. In a separate dish, combine the lime juice, black pepper, coriander, 1 tbsp of chopped garlic, and half of the olive oil. Marinate the chicken breasts in this mixture for 6 to 8 hours or overnight in the refrigerator.

3. On a lightly greased grill over medium-high heat, barbecue the flank steak for 3 to 5 minutes per side, or until desired doneness is reached. Then barbecue the chicken for 5 to 6 minutes per side until the chicken is completely done.

4. Heat the remaining olive oil in a medium-sized fry pan over high heat. Sauté the peppers, onion and 2 tbsp of chopped garlic for 3 to 5 minutes until tender.

5. Slice chicken and steak thinly on the bias. Serve with the pepper onion mixture, warmed flour tortillas, grated Monterey Jack cheese, salsa, sour cream, and guacamole.

SERVES 6 TO 8.

BARBECUE PIZZA

YOU'VE HEARD THE AD LINE, "30 MINUTES OR IT'S FREE";
WELL, HERE ARE TWO PIZZAS YOU CAN HAVE READY IN 15 MINUTES OR LESS. THE
KEY IS USING PRE-COOKED PIZZA CRUST OR DOUGH AVAILABLE IN MOST STORES. IT
COOKS LIKE A PIZZA OVEN, BUT YOU GET THE ACCENTS OF THE GRILL— A LITTLE BIT
OF SMOKINESS, A DRY AND CRISPY CRUST. IT CAN BE SERVED HOT OR COLD.

Pesto

4 oz	toasted pine nuts
1/4 cup	chopped garlic
2 bunches	cleaned basil
1/2 cup	olive oil
75 g	Parmesan cheese
	salt and pepper to taste

In a large food processor mix all ingredients to a paste.

PESTO GOAT CHEESE PIZZA

1 lb	pizza dough, or 2 pre-cooked pizza crusts
1/2 cup	pesto, spread evenly
1/2 cup	goat cheese, spread evenly
1/4 cup	sliced sundried tomatoes
1/8 cup	Reggianno Parmesan, grated
8	opal basil leaves

1. If using pizza dough, roll out 2 10-inch rounds and pre-cook in oven or barbeque.

2. Over medium-heat in the barbecue, brush the pre-cooked pizza crusts with 1 tbsp olive oil.

3. Bake for 2 minutes top side down until heated. Remove and add the toppings.

4. Close cover on barbecue and bake over medium low heat for 5 to 7 minutes until cheese melts.

CHICKEN CLUB PIZZA

1 lb	pizza dough or 2 pre-cooked pizza crusts
1 cup	sliced fully cooked chicken breast
1/2 cup	pre-cooked bacon
1	sliced tomato
1/2 cup	salsa
1	small sliced red onion
1	green pepper, roasted and sliced
1 cup	cheddar cheese, grated
1/2 cup	mozzarella cheese, grated

Follow instructions for Pesto Goat Cheese Pizza.

Serves 8 to 10.

MUSHROOM, CHICKEN ASIAGO TORTILLA TORE

	7" spring form pan
3	6 oz chicken breasts fully cooked on the grill and then sliced
2 cups	Sitake mushrooms, thinly sliced
1 medium	sweet white onion, thinly sliced
2 tbsp	olive oil
2 tbsp	chopped fresh herbs (basil, thyme, oregano, rosemary)
1 cup	asiago cheese, grated
2 cups	old white cheddar cheese, grated
5	7" flour tortillas
5 tbsp	bechamel sauce
2 tbsp	olive oil for grilling the tortilla torte

1. Sauté the mushrooms and onions over medium heat in the oil for 6-8 minutes until tender. Mix the mushrooms and onion with the julienned chicken and chopped herbs. Season with salt and pepper and set aside.

2. To assemble, place one tortilla in the bottom of the spring form pan. Top with one tablespoon of bechamel sauce and spread evenly. Top with a quarter of the chicken, mushroom, onion, and herb mixture. For the next layer evenly sprinkle a quarter of the cheese onto the top of the chicken mixture. Cover with another tortilla and repeat layers until all of the ingredients are used up.

3. Wrap tightly with plastic wrap and place a heavy weight on top. Refrigerate for 6-8 hours, or overnight.

4. Remove weight, plastic wrap and the springform pan. Cut into 8 wedges and bake on a cookie sheet at 400 degree F. for 15 minutes or until edges are bubbly and the outside are golden brown. You may also grill each of the wedges over medium heat. Brush all sides of the wedges and grill for 10-12 minutes turning gently on all sides, until golden brown and warm through.

5. Serve with warmed tomato sauce.

MAKES 8 SERVINGS.

CHICKEN WINGS

═══════════

CHICKEN WINGS: IT ALL STARTED AT THE ANCHOR BAR IN BUFFALO.
EVERYONE LOVES WINGS; THEY'RE A GREAT AS A SNACK OR ON A PICNIC, COOL OR
HOT. HERE ARE TWO TASTY RECIPES. MAKE SURE YOU USE A BARBECUE BASKET
WHEN YOU GRILL WINGS OR THEY'LL FALL THROUGH THE GRILL.

═══════════

TEQUILA BARBECUE CHICKEN WINGS

1/4 cup	tequila
2 tbsp	lemon juice
2 tbsp	red wine vinegar
3 tbsp	chopped garlic
1/4 cup	vegetable oil
1/2 cup	oyster sauce
to taste	salt and freshly ground black pepper
3/4 cup	maple syrup
10 lbs	chicken wings (tips removed and cut in half to give you drumsticks and flats)

1. In a mixing bowl whisk together everything except the chicken wings.

2. Place wings in a large, thick zipper-lock plastic bag with the marinade. Marinate refrigerated 6 to 8 hours or overnight.

3. Remove wings from bag and, on a lightly greased grill, barbecue over medium to medium-high heat for 12 to 15 minutes, turning and basting (with reserved marinade) frequently until done, golden brown and crispy. Serve with Blue Cheese Dip, page 19.

SERVES 10 TO 12.

HONEY GARLIC JUMBO CHICKEN WINGS

4 lbs	jumbo chicken wings, trimmed and separated
4 tbsp	chopped garlic
1/2 cup	honey
1/4 cup	rice vinegar
1/4 cup	vegetable oil
3 tbsp	soya sauce
1 tsp	salt
2 tsp	black pepper
1 tsp	mustard powder
1 tsp	cinnamon
1 tsp	cumin
1 tbsp	chopped fresh thyme
2 tbsp	sesame seeds

1. Mix together thoroughly the garlic, honey, rice vinegar, oil, soya sauce, salt, pepper, mustard, cinnamon, cumin, thyme and sesame seeds.

2. Place chicken wings in a large bowl. Cover with marinade and refrigerate for 4-6 hours or overnight.

3. Preheat oven to 400°F.

4. Arrange wings on a foil-covered baking sheet.

5. Bake for 15-20 minutes.

6. Remove chicken wings from the oven and grill, turning frequently, over medium heat for 10-15 minutes until lightly charred and crisp.

SERVES 8 TO 10 FOR A CROWD-PLEASING MESS OF WINGS.

SPICY JERK CHICKEN WITH RUM PLANTAINS ON SUGAR CANE SKEWERS

4	skinless chicken breasts
5g	jerk paste (page 31)
1 stalk	sugar cane
1 1/4 cup	pineapple juice
2	ripe plantains
2 tbsp	dark rum
1 oz	brown sugar
	olive oil

1. Cut each chicken breast into 6 bite-size cubes.

2. Marinate with jerk paste overnight.

3. Cut the husk off the sugar cane into 6-inch long, 1/2-inch wide strips making a point at one end.

4. Soak sugar cane skewers in pineapple juice overnight.

5. Remove skin from ripe plantains. Cut plantains into 24 mini logs.

6. Place plantains in mixing bowl and toss together with dark rum and brown sugar; marinate for 20 minutes.

7. Place plantain on skewers, followed by jerk chicken.

8. Brush lightly with olive oil.

9. Grill on barbecue over medium heat.

SERVES 6 (24 SKEWERS).

SPICY CHICKEN JERK PASTE

This jerk paste is a recipe we use at home. It's from Bridgette's grandmother who's from Spanishtown, Jamaica.

6	green onions, chopped
1	scotch bonnet pepper, whole with seeds
2	spanish onions, chopped
1/4 cup	soy sauce
4 twigs	fresh thyme (use leaves only)
1 tsp	olive oil

Mix all ingredients in food processor until smooth paste is formed.

Makes 1 1/2 cups

SEARED SHERRY AND BEET-MARINATED SALMON ON BELGIAN ENDIVE WITH PEPPERED MANGO

12 oz	salmon fillet (center cut)
	zest of one lemon
4 sprigs	dill
1/2 lb.	beets, finely puréed
1 tsp	salt
1 tsp	sugar
2 oz	sherry
20 leaves	basil
8 sprigs	thyme
1/2	mango
	cracked black pepper
1/2 cup	citrus vinaigrette
2 spears	Belgian endive

Garnish:

chervil

chives

beet oil

1. Place salmon on tray, skin-side down.

2. Sprinkle salmon with lemon zest and dill. Pack on beet purée. Sprinkle with salt and sugar. Splash finely with sherry.

3. Cover salmon with cling film. Place another tray on top and press with heavy weights.

4. Refrigerate salmon for 24 hours.

5. Remove salmon from fridge. Remove beet mixture.

6. Cut salmon into four squares. Slice each square into five slices.

7. Layer each slice with a basil leaf and put back together with skewers of thyme sprigs.

8. Cut mango into a small chunks and season with cracked black pepper.

9. Toss peppered mango in a little citrus vinaigrette — lemon, lime juice and olive oil.

10. Cut endive into a fine julienne and toss in citrus vinaigrette; season to taste.

11. Sear salmon on a hot, oiled pan skin-side down until crisp; turn salmon over and sear the flesh side, keeping the salmon rare.

12. Pack endive into a ring; place salmon on top. Spoon peppered mango around salmon. Garnish with beet oil and fresh herbs.

SERVES 4.

SALADS

ASIAGO ASPARAGUS SALAD

A DELICIOUS COMBO OF TENDER SWEET ASPARAGUS AND THE BEAUTIFUL PUNGENCY

OF ASIAGO CHEESE... FAST AND SIMPLE TO PREPARE.

ASPARAGUS IS A REAL SPRING SUMMER VEGETABLE.

2	bunches of asparagus
1/4 cup	chopped shallots
	freshly ground black pepper to taste
1 cup	grated asiago cheese
1/2 cup	red wine vinegar
1 tbsp	chopped fresh sage
	salt to taste
1 cup	olive oil

1. Peel and trim the asparagus. Blanch for 4 minutes. Cool after blanching.

2. Mix remaining ingredients together to make the dressing

3. Pour dressing over the blanched asparagus.

4. Chill for 1 to 2 hours before serving.

SERVES 4 TO 6.

ASPARAGUS, ONION AND PEPPER SALAD

SERVE THIS SALAD WITH THE OVEN-ROASTED MUSSELS AND CLAMS ON PAGE 102.

1 each	red, orange, yellow peppers
1 bunch	asparagus, trimmed
1	bulb onion, whites only

Dressing:

1/2 cup	red wine vinegar
3 tbsp	shallots, finely chopped
1/3 cup	honey
1/4 cup	fresh chopped thyme
1 tbsp	low-sodium seasoning
3 tbsp	olive oil
	salt and pepper to taste

1. Cut the peppers into 1-inch slices

2. Trim the asparagus and blanch. Cut into 1-inch slices

3. Cut the white of the bulb onion into thin slices

4. Combine all the dressing ingredients in a bowl, adjusting seasoning to taste.

5. Toss the dressing and vegetables together in a large bowl, then transfer to serving bowl or platter.

SERVES 4.

RED BEET AND SWEET ONION SALAD

6 large	red beets, fully cooked, cooled and peeled
1 medium	sweet onion live a Vidalia or Texas or Maui, sliced thinly
2	green onions, sliced thinly
1 tbsp	Pommery mustard
3 tbsp	olive oil
1 tbsp	red wine vinegar
2 tbsp	orange juice
1 tbsp	chopped dill
	salt and pepper to taste

1. Slice the beets into 1/4 inch thick rounds. Add sweet onions, green onions, pommery mustard, olive oil, red wine vinegar, orange juice and dill. Season with salt and pepper to taste.

2. Cover and refrigerate and serve.

SERVES 4

FENNEL AND MUSHROOM SALAD

1 lb	cremini brown mushrooms, sliced
2 tbsp	vegetable oil
2 heads	fresh fennel, julienned
1	large red onion, sliced
1 bunch	green onion, sliced
	salt and freshly ground black pepper to taste

Vinaigrette:

1/4 cup	Dijon mustard
1/4 cup	red wine vinegar
1/2 cup	olive oil
2 tbsp	chopped fresh dill
1 tbsp	cracked black pepper
1	whole red bell pepper, finely diced

1. In a medium-sized fry pan over medium-high heat, sauté the mushrooms in the vegetable oil for 3 to 5 minutes until slightly tender.

2. To make the vinaigrette, whisk together the Dijon mustard, vinegar, dill, olive oil, red pepper and cracked black pepper.

3. Mix the dressing with the fennel, red onion, sautéed mushrooms, green onion, and salt and pepper to taste.

4. Chill for 1 to 2 hours, and serve.

SERVES 4 TO 6.

FIREWORKS COLESLAW

I USED TO MAKE THIS AT A RESTAURANT CALLED PERRY'S. TRADITIONAL COLESLAW IS
USUALLY SWEET AND CRUNCHY. THIS ONE IS FULL OF SPICY COLOR AND ZING.
IT'S A GREAT ACCOMPANIMENT FOR GRILLED CHICKEN, PAN-FRIED BASS OR PICKEREL.

1	medium-sized white cabbage, thinly sliced
1 each	red, yellow, orange and green peppers, julienned 2 inches x 1/4 inch thick
1/2 cup	chopped fresh parsley
1/4 cup	chopped fresh coriander
2	medium-sized carrots trimmed, peeled and grated

Mix all the ingredients together. Toss with the Spiced Dressing.

Spiced Dressing:

1 1/2 cups	mayonnaise
1/4 cup	red wine vinegar
1/8 cup	lime juice
	salt and pepper to taste
2	finely chopped habeñera (volcanic) chili peppers
1 tsp	mustard powder
1 tbsp	Louisiana hot sauce

Mix all the ingredients thoroughly. Chill for 1 to 2 hours so that the flavors may
blend. Season and serve. Yow-wee!

SERVES 10 TO 12.

SNOW PEA, CAULIFLOWER AND BEAN SALAD

1 cup	snow peas, tops removed
1 head	cauliflower, cut into florets, blanched for 2 minutes
1 cup	green beans, trimmed blanched for 3 minutes
1 cup	yellow beans, trimmed, blanched for 3 minutes

Buttermilk Dressing:

1/2 cup	mayonnaise
1/4 cup	sour cream
2 tbsp	buttermilk
1 tbsp	fresh chopped basil
1 tbsp	fresh chopped parsley
1 tbsp	fresh chopped garlic

1. In a large service bowl arrange vegetables as desired.

2. In a mixing bowl, combine all the dressing ingredients. Adjust seasoning to taste.

3. Pour the dressing over the vegetables.

SERVES 4 TO 6

GRILLED GREEK SALAD

A TASTE OF THE GREEK ISLANDS ON YOUR VERY OWN

COTTAGE DOCK OR BACKYARD DECK.

1/4 cup	olive oil
2 tbsp	red wine vinegar
1 tbsp	lemon juice
1 tbsp each	chopped garlic, oregano and parsley
	salt and pepper to taste
1 medium	red onion, slice into 4 rounds
1 each	red, yellow and green pepper, cut into 4 wedges
1 large	field tomato, cut into 4 rounds 1/2 inch thick
8 slices	English cucumber 1/4 inch thick
2 tbsp	olive oil
2 tbsp	red wine vinegar
4 slices	Greek Feta cheese, cut into 2 x 2 inch cubes
12	dry cured black olives
	baby lettuce for garnish

1. To make the dressing mix together the olive oil, red wine vinegar, lemon juice, garlic, oregano, and parsley and season to taste with salt and pepper.

2. Toss the red onion, red, yellow and green peppers, tomato, and cucumber, with olive oil, red wine vinegar.

3. Place the vegetables in a well-greased grill over medium-high heat and cook for 5-7 minutes until lightly charred and tender. Set aside.

4. Season the cheese with black pepper and place on the grill. Heat just until soft, about 3 minutes turning once.

5. To assemble salad equally divide the vegetables among 4 plates starting with the tomato on the bottom then the red onion, next the cucumber slices and finish with 1 wedge of each colored pepper. Set the warm cheese on top and garnish with a small bunch of baby lettuce and 3 black olives.

6. Drizzle dressing over top and serve.

SERVES 4.

GREEN BEAN & BACON SALAD

TENDER GREEN BEANS AND SMOKY BACON TOSSED IN A

CREAMY BUTTERMILK DRESSING.

2 lbs	green beans, trimmed and blanched then cooled
2 cups	multi-colored sweet peppers, julienned
1 cup	spanish onion, sliced
1 cup	julienned celery root
1/2 lb	diced bacon, sautéed until crispy and drained of fat

Dressing:

1 cup	buttermilk
1/2 cup	sour cream
1/4 cup	chopped shallot
2 tbsp	olive oil
1/4 cup	Dijon mustard
3 tbsp	chopped fresh tarragon
	salt and freshly ground black pepper to taste

1. In a mixing bowl, whisk together the buttermilk, sour cream, shallot, olive oil, Dijon mustard, and tarragon.

2. Mix all of the remaining ingredients together with the buttermilk dressing. Season and toss.

3. Chill for 1 to 2 hours before serving.

SERVES 4 TO 6.

TUSCAN BREAD SALAD WITH GRILLED PEPPERS AND ZUCCHINI

SALAD IS NOT JUST LETTUCE, AS THIS RECIPE DEMONSTRATES.

1	day-old crusty Italian-style white bread
1/4 cup	extra virgin olive oil
3	red bell peppers (cut in 1 inch strips)
1	zucchini, diced
1/2 cup	100% maple syrup
2 tsp	fresh lemon juice
1 tsp	dried basil
2 bunches	arugula (coarse stems removed)

1. Slice bread in half lengthwise.

2. Brush bread over with some of the oil and place on the grill over medium-high heat, turning often, until lightly browned all over. Cut each bread strip into 2-inch cubes. Set aside.

3. In medium-size bowl, combine red peppers and zucchini. Add maple syrup, 2 tbsp of olive oil, lemon juice and basil and toss. Let vegetables marinate for 20 to 30 minutes.

4. Place peppers and zucchini in grill basket, reserving marinade. Place on grill over medium-high heat and cook about 8 to 12 minutes or until lightly charred, turning carefully every few minutes.

5. In bowl, combine grill vegetables, bread cubes and reserved marinade. Toss lightly with salt and pepper and serve

SERVES 4 TO 6.

GRILLED CAESAR SALAD

Every cooking show I've seen and every restaurant I've been to serves caesar salad. This is the cottage country way of doing a caesar salad. You grill everything from the lettuce to the bread to the garlic. The anchovies for the dressing can be grilled as well.

1 head	romaine lettuce, cleaned and cut in half
2 heads	Belgian endive, cut in half
1 head	radicchio, cleaned and cut in half
12 slices	french stick (1/2-inch thick)
8 slices	bacon
1/4 cup	coarsely grated parmesan
	salt and pepper to taste

1. Toss romaine, endive and radicchio in salt and pepper and olive oil.

2. Grill for 2 to 3 minutes per side over medium heat. Grill french bread and bacon for same amount of time or until crispy

3. Cut lettuce halves in half again.

4. Arrange on plate and then top with bacon and grilled toast

5. Drizzle with dressing (recipe follows) and parmesan cheese.

Caesar Salad Dressing:

8 cloves	garlic
5 tbsp	olive oil
1 tbsp	lemon juice
2 tbsp	red wine vinegar
2 tbsp	Dijon mustard
3 tbsp	chopped anchovy (tinned is just fine but fresh is even better)
	salt and ground black pepper to taste

1. Poach the garlic in boiling water for 3 minutes.

2. Grill the poached garlic until slightly charred.

3. Mix garlic with remaining ingredients.

SERVES 4.

GRILLED FENNEL AND PANCETTA SALAD

THE BEAUTIFUL LICORICE SWEETNESS OF FENNEL BLENDED

WITH CURED ITALIAN BACON.

3	large fennel bulbs
	salt and pepper to taste
6 tbsp	olive oil
12 slices	pancetta (have your deli slice this thin and placed individually on wax paper, not touching or overlapping as they will stick together)
1	red onion, thinly sliced
1 cup	black olives
1	large lime, juiced
1/4 cup	grated parmesan cheese

1. Trim the tops and bottoms of the fennel bulbs. Cut them lengthwise into 1/2-inch slices (12 slices total).

2. Season the fennel slices with salt, pepper and olive oil (about 1 tsp of oil per slice of fennel).

3. Over medium high heat, grill the fennel until slightly charred and tender turning twice (approximately 5 to 6 minutes). Set aside.

4. Grill the pancetta over low to medium heat until crispy.

5. Arrange the fennel and pancetta on a plate alternating each slice. Top with slices of red onion and olives.

6. Mix the lime juice and olive oil and drizzle over the salad.

7. Top with grated parmesan cheese and serve.

SERVES 6 TO 8.

GRILLED VEGETABLE SALAD

THIS IS MY FAVORITE. USE ANY KIND OF VEGETABLES YOU WANT. THIS MAKES A GREAT ANTIPASTO, SALAD, OR VEGETABLE WITH YOUR MAIN COURSE.

1 cup	baby yellow squash
1 cup	baby green zucchini
1 cup	marrow, sliced , 1/4-inch thick
1 cup	yellow summer zucchini, sliced 1/4" thick
1 cup	asparagus, peeled and trimmed (approx. 12 pieces)
3 cups	rainbow peppers, seeded and sliced into 2 x 2 inch wedges
1	medium red onion, sliced
1	baby eggplant, sliced 1/4-inch thick
1 cup	shiitake mushrooms, stems removed
1 cup	oyster mushrooms, torn into 1-inch thick pieces
1 tbsp	barbecue spice seasoning
2 tbsp	chopped fresh thyme
1/4 cup	extra virgin olive oil
2 tbsp	chopped fresh garlic

Vinaigrette:

1/2 cup	extra virgin olive oil
1/4 cup	balsamic vinegar
2 tbsp	Dijon mustard
1 tbsp	chopped thyme

Garnish:

1/2 cup	Niçoise black olives
1/2 cup	caper berries, stem removed (or capers)

1. Preheat the barbecue to medium high.

2. Place all prepared vegetables in a large bowl. Add barbecue seasoning spice, garlic, thyme and olive oil. Toss well, so that all vegetables become covered with the mixture.

3. Place the vegetables into a barbecue basket, secure the lid of the basket. Grill for 10-12 minutes per side or until the vegetables are tender and slightly charred.

4. Mix all the vinaigrette ingredients and whisk lightly.

5. Pour vegetables from the grill basket into a large bowl. Add olives, caper berries and vinaigrette. Toss well and serve.

SERVES 8 TO 10.

MACARONI AND CHEESE SALAD

I CAME UP WITH THIS WHEN I WAS WORKING FOR A CATERING COMPANY. KIDS LOVE MACARONI AND CHEESE, AND THIS SALAD HAS LOADS OF CHEESE FLAVOR.

2 cups	dried macaroni
1 cup	grated fresh carrot
2 cups	grated cheddar cheese/yellow medium-aged
1 cup	chopped green onion
1/4 cup	chopped parsley
1 cup	mayonnaise
1/4 cup	Dijon mustard
1 tbsp	paprika
	salt and pepper to taste

1. Cook the macaroni according to the directions on the package. Allow to cool.

2. Mix all of the remaining ingredients with the fully cooked macaroni. Chill and serve.

SERVES 6 TO 8.

POTATO SALAD

This is my mother's version of potato salad, so it's very close to my heart.

2 lb	Yukon Gold potatoes, peeled and diced in 1 1/2 inch cubes
1/2 cup	stone-ground mustard
1/2 cup	green onion, chopped
1 cup	Spanish onion, chopped into 1/4-inch cubes
3 cups	Granny Smith apples, cored and diced in 1/2-inch cubes
1/4 cup	fresh dill, chopped
1 1/4 cups	mayonnaise
	salt and pepper to taste

1. Place potatoes and a teaspoon of salt in a medium-sized pot and fill to covering with cold water. Place on high heat and bring to a boil.

2. Turn heat to medium-low and let the potatoes simmer for approximately 15-20 minutes, until they are tender but not mushy. Drain and let cool.

3. Once the potatoes have cooled, add onion, green onions, mustard, apple, mayonnaise, dill and seasoning.

4. Mix well and chill for 1 hour before serving.

SERVES 6 TO 8.

POTATO CAULIFLOWER SALAD

3 small	Yukon Gold potatoes,
1 small head	cauliflower
1/2	red onion, cut into 1/2-inch slices
2 cups	sugar snap peas, tops trimmed
	shaved Parmesan pieces
	Green Goddess Dressing (recipe follows)

1. Blanch the potatoes for 7-9 minutes, dry, then cut into wedges.

2. Cut the cauliflower into small florets, blanch and dry.

3. Arrange vegetables on a platter or in a glass bowl. Drizzle Green Goddess dressing over top. Top with Parmesan.

Green Goddess Dressing:

1/3 cup	mayonnaise
1/3 cup	sour cream
1	green onion, finely sliced
1 tbsp	vinegar
1/3 cup	fresh chopped basil
1 tsp	chopped fresh garlic
1/3 cup	fresh chopped tarragon
1/2 cup	fresh chopped parsley
	salt and pepper

In a mixing bowl, combine all ingredients together, adjust seasoning, and pour over the vegetables.

SERVES 4 TO 6.

SOUR SLAW

A CLASSIC COLESLAW.

1	medium-sized green cabbage (core removed and finely sliced).
1	finely sliced medium Spanish onion
3 tbsp	chopped parsley
1/4 cup	white vinegar
1/3 cup	vegetable canola oil
1 tbsp	sugar
1/2 tsp	salt
1 tsp	freshly ground black pepper

Mix all of the ingredients and let stand 1 hour before serving.

SERVES 8 TO 10.

TEXAS CAVIAR SALAD

A NEW TWIST ON BEANS— A FUN BEAN SALAD.

2 cups	dried black-eyed peas
4 cups	water
1/2 tsp	salt

1. Rinse the peas in a colander and pick out any stones or debris. Soak them overnight in 3 times in volume.

2. Drain the peas, discard water, and put in a large stock pot. Add water and salt. Bring to a boil, reduce the heat to simmer, cover and cook for 45 minutes. Remove the cover and cook for 45 minutes to 1 hour, or until they are tender. Strain and rinse under cold water until cool.

3. In a large bowl combine the peas with the garnish and vinaigrette ingredients (ingredients to follow). Mix well and let stand refrigerated for 1 hour.

4. Season to taste and serve.

Garnish:

1 cup	chopped green onion
1 cup	chopped red pepper
1	chopped fresh jalapeño pepper, seeds and stem removed
1 cup	chopped yellow pepper
1 tbsp	chopped cilantro
1 tbsp	chopped parsley
1 cup	grated carrot
1 cup	corn (fresh kernels or packaged, thawed and drained)

Vinaigrette:

2 tbsp	freshly squeezed lime juice
2 tbsp	freshly squeezed lemon juice
2 tbsp	freshly squeezed orange juice
1/4 cup	olive oil
1 tbsp	chopped garlic
1/4 tsp	cayenne pepper
1 tbsp	honey
to taste	salt and freshly ground pepper

SERVES 6 TO 8.

POTATO AND CORN SALAD WITH YOGURT DRESSING

HERE'S ANOTHER VERSION OF CLASSIC POTATO SALAD

2 lb	small red or white potatoes, quartered
1 1/2 cups	corn kernels
1/2 cup	yogurt
1 cup	chopped green onion
2 tbsp	white vinegar
1 tbsp	chopped thyme
1 tbsp	olive oil
3 tbsp	Pommery mustard
1	medium leek, chopped
	salt and pepper to taste

1. In a large saucepan of boiling water cook potatoes until tender, 8-10 minutes. Drain well.

2. In a large skillet, heat oil until hot and cook corn, shaking skillet until slightly browned, about 3 minutes. Cool corn and potatoes.

3. In a bowl stir together cooked potatoes, corn and remaining ingredients. Season and serve.

SERVES 4 TO 6.

SUMMER BARLEY SALAD

BARLEY IS NOT JUST FOR SOUP ANY MORE. IT GIVES THIS SALAD A NUTTY FLAVOR.

1 tsp	salt
1 cup	quick-cooking barley
1 cup	diced red pepper
1 tsp	cumin
1 tsp	chopped oregano
1 tsp	hot sauce
2 tbsp	olive oil
2 tbsp	chopped cilantro
3 tbsp	lime juice
1/3 cup	tomato juice
1 cup	diced red onion
2 cup	frozen baby peas

1. In a medium saucepan, bring 3 cups of water and salt to a boil.

2. Add the barley and cook until tender (about 10 minutes).

3. Drain and rinse the barley under cold water. Press the barley to remove excess moisture.

4. Transfer barley to a bowl and add all the remaining ingredients. Mix, season, chill for 1 hour and serve.

SERVES 6 TO 8.

MEATS

BARBECUE ROAST OF PRIME RIB

12 lb	roast of prime rib
1/2 cup	low-sodium seasoning
Devil Barbecue Sauce (recipe follows)	

1. Preheat barbecue to high heat for 10 minutes.

2. Rub seasoning into entire surface of roast.

3. Thread roast onto rotisserie spit and secure.

4. Place onto rotisserie motor. Sear the roast for 15-20 minutes.

5. Reduce heat to medium and roast for approximately 3 hours.

6. Remove from heat; slide off spit; let stand for 5 minutes.

7. Slice to desired-size cuts.

8. Baste roast with Devil Barbecue Sauce.

Devil Barbecue Sauce:

1 1/2 cup	hickory barbecue sauce
3 tbsp	jarred or freshly grated horseradish
1/2 cup	fresh chopped thyme, parsley, basil
1 tbsp	vegetable or olive oil
1/3 cup	Bourbon whiskey
	freshly ground black pepper

Combine all ingredients in a mixing bowl. Season with black pepper.

SERVES 8 TO 10.

COLOSSAL BARBECUE BEEF KEBABS

MOST KEBABS I'VE HAD ARE WELL-DONE, TOUGH AND DRIED OUT, SO I DECIDED TO

MAKE KEBABS THAT ARE HUGE, BIG CHUNKS OF MEAT ON HUGE SKEWERS.

THEY LOOK COLOSSAL AND TASTE PHENOMENAL.

2 lb	sirloin steak (1 1/2 to 2-inches thick)
1	large red onion
1	sweet red pepper
1	sweet yellow pepper
1	sweet green pepper
1	medium-sized eggplant
24	mushroom caps (medium-sized field or cremini will do)

1. Cut the beef into 1 1/2 to 2-inch cubes. Cut the onion, sweet peppers and the eggplant into similar-sized chunks.

2. Alternately thread the steak, mushrooms, onions, and sweet pepper onto long metal skewers. Brush with 1/2 of the marinade (recipe on page 63) and let stand for 2 hours.

3. Place the colossal kebabs on a greased grill over medium-high heat. Cook, turning and basting occasionally with the marinade for 8 to 10 minutes or until the beef is medium rare and the vegetables are tender and slightly charred.

4. Remove from the grill. Baste with a little more marinade and season to taste with salt and pepper. Serve with reserved marinade, barbecue Greek-style pita and minty tzatziki sauce (recipe on page 140).

SERVES 6 TO 8.

GRILLED DOUBLE-THICK CUT LAMB CHOPS

TEQUILA ADDS THE FLAVOR OF THE CACTUS. THIS IS BASICALLY MARGARITA LAMB
(BUT IT DOESN'T DO THE MACARENA).

9	double-thick cut lamb chops, bones frenched (Ask the butcher to do the frenching for you.)

Marinade:

2 tbsp	chopped fresh rosemary
2 tbsp	chopped fresh garlic
1/4 cup	fresh lime juice
1/4 cup	tequila
1 tbsp	Dijon mustard
1 tbsp	honey
1 tbsp	freshly ground pepper
1/4 cup	extra virgin olive oil

1. Mix all the marinade ingredients together and pour over the lamb chops. Marinate 4-6 hours or overnight, turning occasionally to keep all the chops in the marinade.

2. Grill lamb chops over high heat to sear in all the juices and flavor. Cook for 3-5 minutes per side for medium rare.

SERVES 3.

COWBOY STEAK

I HAD MY FIRST COWBOY STEAK AT RED SAGE RESTAURANT IN WASHINGTON, D.C.

IN 1991. MY THANKS TO MARK MILLER, ONE OF THE HOTTEST U.S. CHEFS.

IT'S THE MOST HEAVENLY STEAK I HAD EVER EATEN IN MY LIFE.

THIS IS MY VERSION, WITH AN ORIENTAL TWIST.

2	bone-in ribeye steaks, each about 16 to 24 oz, and 2 inches thick
1/4 cup	chopped garlic
1 tbsp	chopped fresh rosemary
1 tbsp	cracked black pepper
1 tbsp	chopped fresh ginger
1/4 cup	soya sauce
1/8 cup	rice wine vinegar
1/8 cup	extra virgin olive oil
1 tsp	sesame seed oil

1. Wipe beef with damp cloth and pat dry.

2. Mix together chopped garlic, rosemary, and black pepper. Rub the steaks all over with the garlic-rosemary mixture.

3. Mix together the ginger, soya sauce-ginger mixture. Let marinate for 30 to 40 minutes.

4. On a lightly greased grill over medium-high heat, cook for 8 to 10 minutes per side for medium rare — or to desired doneness.

5. Allow hot meat to cool for 5 minutes. Slice, and serve with Balsamic Red Onions, and Grilled New Potatoes (page 123).

SERVES 4.

MEXICAN PEPPERED STEAK

ANOTHER WAY TO DO GREAT STEAKS ON THE BARBECUE. I WAS IN MEXICO IN 1989.
I WENT TO A RESTAURANT IN AN OLD OLD BUILDING IN MEXICO CITY WHERE I WAS
SERVED A DELICIOUS STEAK. THE MEAT WAS TENDER AND THE FLAVORS ON THE
OUTSIDE WERE HOT AND ZESTY. I HAVE MODIFIED THEM FOR MY OWN VERSION.

1 tbsp	lime juice
4 tbsp	coarsely ground black pepper
1 tsp	cumin
4 tbsp	chopped garlic
3 to 6 pces	coarsely ground dried chipotle chili (or any other chili pepper will do)
1 tsp	ground coriander
4 tbsp	spiced chili oil (or vegetable oil)
8	8-oz New York strip loin steaks (the best grade you can find)
8 slices	3-oz slices Monterey Jack cheese
8	corn tortillas

1. In a bowl mix together the lime juice, black pepper, cumin, chopped garlic, chipotle chili, ground coriander with 1 tbsp of the spiced chili oil.

2. Coat each steak on both sides with the spice mixture. Let the steaks marinate for 1 hour.

3. Over medium heat, barbecue the steaks approximately 3 to 4 minutes per side for medium doneness.

4. When the steaks are just about done to your likeness, top each with a slice of cheese. Turn to low and close the lid until the cheese melts.

5. Brush the tortillas with the remaining spiced oil and grill for approximately 30 second per side until crispy. Serve with the steak.

SERVES 8.

BARBECUE LAMB STEAK WITH BLUE CHEESE CRUST

1/4 cup	fresh chopped garlic
1/4 cup	bourbon
1/4 cup	maple syrup
1/4 cup	dry herbs (rosemary, oregano, thyme)
1/4 cup	olive oil
1 tbsp	freshly milled black pepper
4	8-oz lamb loins
4	Blue Cheese Crust patties (recipe follows)

1. Combine first 6 ingredients in a bowl.

2. Arrange the lamb in a shallow glass dish and cover with the marinade. Cover and marinate in the fridge overnight (24 hours for best results).

3. Preheat grill to medium high heat.

4. Place marinated lamb loins on grill and cook for 12-15 minutes, turning once.

5. Place the Blue Cheese Crust patties on the loins.

6. Close the lid of the barbecue, reduce the temperature to low. Allow cheese crust to melt, approximately 5-10 minutes.

Blue Cheese Crust

1 cup	blue cheese, softened
1/2 cup	caramelized onions
1/4 cup	fresh herbs (rosemary, parsley)
3 tbsp	breadcrumbs
3 tbsp	olive oil

1. Combine all ingredients in a mixing bowl.

2. Shape mixture into 4 patties to sit on the lamb loins for melting.

SERVES 4.

MONTREAL SPICE-RUBBED BEEF TENDERLOIN

WITH SMOKY CEDAR-PLANKED ONION BARBECUE SAUCE

THIS IS A CLASSIC CANADIAN-SEASONED STEAK, FAMOUS IN QUEBEC. IT HAS AS ITS MAIN INGREDIENT IS PICKLING SPICE. YOU CRACK THE PICKLING SPICE ONTO THE MEAT AND THEN GRILL IT UP. THE FLAVOR IT GIVES ARE IS JUST INCREDIBLE.

1/4 cup	pickling spice, cracked
1 tbsp	coarse sea salt
2 tbsp	cracked black pepper
2 tbsp	chopped garlic
1 tbsp	chopped fresh herbs (rosemary, thyme, oregano)
6	8-oz aged AAA Alberta beef tenderloin filets
2 tbsp	olive oil
3 cups	cedar-planked onions, chopped (page 84)
2 oz	Bourbon whisky
2 oz	demi glace
1 cup	hickory barbecue sauce
1 tbsp	prepared horseradish
	salt and pepper to taste

1. Mix together first 5 ingredients and rub all over the steaks, pressing the spice into the meat.

2. In a medium saucepan, heat the oil over medium high heat; add the cedar-planked onions and sauté for 2 minutes.

3. Deglaze with the Bourbon whisky.

4. Add the demi-glace and barbecue sauce.

5. Bring to a boil, reduce heat to low and let simmer, stirring occasionally, for 15 minutes.

6. Finish with the horseradish.

SERVES 6.

SPICY BARBECUE SHORT RIBS

This is a variation on Miami ribs with a hot and sweet barbecue sauce.

5 lb	beef short ribs, cut 1-inch thick
2 tbsp	mustard seeds
2 tbsp	coarse-cracked black pepper
2 tsp	hot chili flakes
	salt to taste
2 cups	barbecue sauce
1/4 cup	Louisiana hot sauce
2 tbsp	chopped garlic
1/4 cup	olive oil
1/4 cup	red wine vinegar
1 tbsp	black pepper
1/4 cup	maple syrup
2 tbsp	chopped cilantro
	salt to taste

1. Mix together the mustard seeds, black pepper and chili flakes.

2. Use mixture to season the meat, pushing the seasoning into the meat. Season to taste with salt. Set aside.

3. To make the sauce, mix together barbecue sauce, Louisiana hot sauce, chopped garlic, olive oil, red wine vinegar, black pepper, maple syrup and cilantro.

4. Preheat the grill to medium high.

5. Brush the ribs with some of the sauce, just enough to lightly coat.

6. Grill the ribs for 5-6 minutes per side until lightly charred and tender.

7. Give the ribs another baste with the sauce and remove from the grill. Serve with the remaining sauce. Serve with Sour Slaw (page 53).

Serves 8.

GRILLED CANADIAN RED DEER VENISON CHOPS

WITH MAPLE MUSTARD BEER BASTE

ON A RECENT EXCURSION TO THE BAYOU OF LOUISIANA, FOUR OTHER CANADIAN CHEFS AND I CREATED A CANADIAN DINNER AT A PLANTATION HOME FOR 150 PEOPLE. WE MADE THIS DISH USING CANADIAN VENISON, QUEBEC MAPLE SYRUP, AND MUSTARD FROM MANITOBA MUSTARD SEEDS. IT WAS SUCCULENT AND TENDER AND A HUGE HIT.

2 tbsp	garlic, chopped
2 tbsp	black pepper, coarsely ground
1 tbsp	rosemary, chopped
1 tbsp	vanilla extract
1 tbsp	thyme, chopped
2 tbsp	olive oil
2 tsp	paprika
1 tbsp	molasses
2 tbsp	balsamic vinegar
6	8-oz Red Deer venison chops

Maple Mustard Beer Baste (recipe follows)

1. Mix first 9 ingredients. Rub thoroughly over venison chops.

2. Let venison marinate in rub for 6-8 hours.

3. On a hot grill over medium high heat, grill the venison for 4-5 minutes per side for medium rare doneness, basting liberally with the Maple Mustard Beer Baste during the last minutes of cooking.

Maple Mustard Beer Baste

1/2 cup	old-fashioned grainy Dijon mustard
1/2 cup	100% pure Canadian maple syrup
1 bottle	strong stout beer

Mix ingredients together.

SERVES 6.

PORK

BARBEQUE PORK TENDERLOIN IN DIJON MUSTARD

VERY SIMPLE, TENDER AND DELICIOUS.

4	pork tenderloin medallions (approximately 3 oz each)
2	oyster mushrooms (or any wild mushroom)
4	Shanghai baby bok choy
2	fresh peaches, halved (with skin)

Marinade

4 tbsp	Dijon mustard
2 tbsp	olive oil
1 tbsp	balsamic vinegar
1 clove	minced garlic

1. Whisk together marinade ingredients; adjust to taste. Pour over uncooked tenderloins and refrigerate for a few hours or overnight.

2. Pre-heat barbecue to high. Place pork tenderloins, oyster mushrooms (face-down at first), bok choy and peaches (flat side down at first) on the barbecue grill. Cover barbecue lid and let cook for 3 to 5 minutes per side.

SERVES 2 TO 4.

GRILLED PORK CHOP WITH PECAN CORNBREAD STUFFING

12 oz	heavy-bodied beer or ale
2 tbsp	vegetable or canola oil
2 tsp	ground fennel seeds
1 tbsp	chopped fresh savory
1 tbsp	chopped fresh garlic
1 tbsp	freshly ground black pepper
2 tbsp	Dijon mustard
6 to 8	frenched pork centre-cut loin chops, 1 1/2 to 2 inches thick

Pecan Cornbread Stuffing (recipe follows)

1. Combine the beer, vegetable oil, fennel, savory, garlic, pepper and mustard and whisk to emulsify.

2. Marinate the pork chops for 1 to 2 hours at room temperature or longer in the refrigerator.

3. Remove the pork chops from the marinade (save the marinade; you will need it for basting later).

4. With a sharp knife slice the pork chop horizontally through the middle of the side. Cut about halfway through forming a pocket.

5. Stuff the cavity with the cornbread stuffing. Put a lot in the cavity— the more stuffing, the greater the chop looks. If you have remaining stuffing roll it in some tin foil and cook it on the barbecue slowly until hot.

6. Over medium high heat on a greased grill, barbecue the pork chops for 5 to 6 minutes per side, basting occasionally with the marinade.

Serve with Texas Caviar Salad (page 54) and Grilled Summer Zucchini (page 117).

SERVES 6 TO 8.

Pecan Cornbread Stuffing

1	small cooking onion, finely chopped
1 tbsp	butter
1 tbsp	olive oil
2 tbsp	chopped fresh savory (sage will do if you don't have savory)
2 cups	unseasoned dried cornbread crumbs (packaged or homemade)
1/2 cup	chopped pecans
1 tbsp	garlic
to taste	salt and pepper
2/3 cup	milk
1 cup	fully cooked and chopped bacon

1. In a small fry pan, sauté the garlic and onion in butter and oil until translucent. Add the savory and stir. Remove from heat.

2. In a large bowl add the cornbread crumbs, stir in the onion mixture, then stir in the milk and bacon.

3. Season to taste with salt and pepper.

BARBECUE
BABY BACK RIBS

Ribs are my passion. I always thought I knew how to cook ribs until
I met Jerry Gibson. Jerry taught me how to cook ribs.
These are the best ribs you'll ever eat. They're so good that Jerry calls
them "ribolicious." Serve these with Fireworks Coleslaw on page 40.

4 racks	fresh baby rack ribs (1 1/2 lb. each), fully trimmed and skinned
1/2 cup	barbeque seasoning
2	lemons, sliced 1/4 inch thick
2 cups	water

1. Season back ribs with the barbeque seasoning. Rub into the meat.

2. Place on a 2-inch deep baking sheet, meat side down. Place 3 to 4 slices of lemon on each rack.

3. Add water to the pan. Cover and bake at 325°F for 1 1/2 hours, or until bone pulls clear from the meat.

4. Remove from oven and pan. Place meat on preheated barbeque grill, and over high heat, char the ribs. Baste with 1/2 cup of barbeque sauce per rack.

5. Remove from grill after the sauce has caramelized.

Serves 4 to 6.

BBQ ASIAN
PORK SPARERIBS

1 tbsp	chopped garlic
1 tsp	chopped fresh ginger
1 tbsp	Chinese hot sauce
3 racks	pork spareribs, approximately 2 lb. each
2	oranges, thinly sliced

Asian BBQ Sauce:

1 cup	Chinese hoisin sauce
3/4 cup	plum sauce
1/4 cup	rice wine vinegar
1/4 cup	fresh squeezed orange juice
1/4 cup	honey
1/4 cup	sherry
1 tsp	sesame oil
1 tbsp	chopped garlic
1 tsp	chopped fresh ginger
3	green onions, finely chopped
	salt and pepper to taste

1. To season the ribs mix together the garlic, ginger and Chinese hot sauce. Rub this mixture all over the spare ribs.

2. Arrange spare ribs meat-side down in a large roasting pan, overlapping as to fit into the pan. Place the orange slice onto each rack of ribs.

3. Cover pan with lid or foil and place in a preheated 325 degree oven for about 1 1/2 hours until the meat pulls away cleanly from the bone.

4. In a medium sauce pan combine the hoisin, plum sauce, rice vinegar, orange juice, honey, sherry, sesame oil, garlic, ginger and green onions. Over medium heat, bring the sauce to a boil and let simmer for 5 minutes. Season to taste with salt and pepper, remove from heat and set aside.

5. Place ribs on a well-seasoned grill over medium-high heat for a few minutes until the ribs are slightly charred and crisp. Continue to cook basting liberally with the reserved sauce, for 5-10 minutes.

6. Remove from the grill and brush again with the sauce and serve.

SERVES 4 TO 6.

PLANK

PLANK SALMON

I LEARNED ABOUT PLANKED SALMON FROM A CHEF FRIEND, REIMER FUHLENDORF.

REIMER USED TO DO PLANKED SALMON IN THE OVEN, SO I MODIFIED THE TECHNIQUE

FOR THE BARBECUE. PLANKED SALMON HAS BECOME MY SIGNATURE DISH.

YOU DON'T HAVE TO USE CEDAR; ANY UNTREATED HARDWOOD WILL WORK.

THE KEY IS TO SOAK THE PLANK.

You will need 1 cedar plank (available at your local lumber yard), 1/2 tp 3/4-inch thick, and 10" x 10" long. Soak the plank overnight in water.

4	5-oz fresh Pacific or Atlantic salmon fillets, skin off
2 tsp	mixed freshly cracked black, white and pink peppercorns
1 tbsp	garlic, chopped
1 tbsp	extra virgin olive oil
2 tsp	fresh lemon juice

1. Mix the lemon juice, olive oil, garlic and peppercorns. Crust the tops of each salmon fillet.

2. Place the cedar plank on preheated 600°F grill. When the wood starts to smoke, approximately 1-2 minutes, place the salmon fillets on the cedar. Close the lid and bake/grill for 12-15 minutes, until the salmon is flaky and pink.

NOTE:
If your cedar plank should catch fire, turn the heat to low and use a spray bottle of water to put the fire out.

SERVES 4.

CEDAR-PLANKED TROUT

HERE'S A CHANGE FROM PAN-FRIED TROUT. PLANKING PROVIDES THE BENEFITS
OF SMOKING WITHOUT THE LONG HOURS SMOKING REQUIRES.

4	whole fresh trout (rainbow, speckle or brown, about 12 - 16 oz each)
1	cedar plank 1/2" x 10" x 12", soaked in water overnight
12	sage leaves
	freshly ground black pepper to taste
4 slices	lemon, halved
2 tbsp	chopped shallots
splash	rum
1 tbsp	sea salt

1. Place 3 sage leaves, 2 lemon half-slices, some shallots, black pepper and a splash of rum inside the cavity of each trout. Season the outside of the trout with salt and pepper and a splash of rum, and get ready to plank!

2. Preheat your barbecue to very, very, very hot.

3. Place cedar plank on grill and close lid. Let the plank start to dry for about 2-3 minutes.

4. Open the barbecue lid. Season plank with sea salt; place the seasoned trout on the plank and close the lid. Cook the trout with the cover down for about 10-12 minutes. If your cedar plank catches fire, turn heat off on one side of the barbecue and put out flames with a squeeze bottle of water and continue cooking.

5. Remove trout form plank and serve with Sage and Pepper Butter (page 145).

SERVES 6 TO 8.

CEDAR PLANK ONIONS

2	cedar planks, soaked for 2 hours in water, or overnight
4 large	Vidalia or other sweet onion
8	garlic cloves, peeled
1-2 tbsp	dry BBQ seasoning

1. Season onion slices generously with BBQ seasoning.

2. Preheat BBQ to very high. Place soaked cedar planks in BBQ and close lid and let wood cook for 3-5 minutes until it starts to crackle. Open lid and place seasoned onions on the cedar planks. Close lid, reduce heat to medium-low, and let onions smoke for 15-20 minutes, turning occasionally, until the onions are slightly charred, smokey and tender.

3. Remove from BBQ and let cool.

MAKES APPROXIMATELY 3 CUPS.

CEDAR-PLANKED BREAST OF CHICKEN
WITH MUSTARD-PECAN CRUST

2	cedar planks, soaked overnight
	sea salt
1 cup	crushed pecans
2 tbsp	pommery mustard
1 tbsp	chopped fresh garlic
6	boneless, skinless chicken breasts

1. Preheat grill to high; set planks on grill and scatter sea salt onto planks.

2. Combine the pecans, mustard and garlic in a mixing bowl, then spread onto the tops of each chicken breast.

3. Arrange breasts on planks. Close the lid of the barbecue. Allow to cook for 18-20 minutes.

4. Remove planks from grill very carefully with a pair of tongs.

5. Gently slide breasts off the planks and transfer to a platter.

SERVES 4 TO 6.

POULTRY

BARBECUE BLACK BEAN QUAIL

QUAIL IS A SMALL GAME BIRD. YOU CAN GET THEM AT A BUTCHER SHOP. ASK THE BUTCHER TO BUTTERFLY THEM. THE FLAVOR OF QUAIL IS STRONGER THAN CHICKEN, PUNGENT AND SWEET. WE'VE GIVEN IT AN ORIENTAL TWIST WITH BLACK BEAN.

1/4 cup	soya sauce
1/4 cup	black bean paste
1 tbsp	chopped garlic
1 tbsp	sesame oil
1/8 cup	rice wine vinegar
1 tbsp	chopped coriander
1 tbsp	chopped fresh ginger
	salt and freshly ground pepper to taste
8	quails, backbones and breast bones removed. (You can easily accomplish this with some kitchen shears, or ask your butcher to do it.)

1. Combine all ingredients except the quails in a bowl.

2. Marinade the quails in the mixture for 4-6 hours.

3. On a lightly greased grill over medium heat, barbecue marinated quail for 3 to 4 minutes per side, until cooked to medium doneness.

Serve with baby greens and Sweet Potato Rosti (page 110).

SERVES 8.

BARBECUE SPATCHCOCK CORNISH HENS

"SPATCHCOCKING" INVOLVES REMOVING THE BACKBONE AND BUTTERFLYING.

SERVE THIS WITH A FENNEL SALAD.

2	Cornish hens (have the butcher "spatchcock" the hens, by removing the backbone, thighbone, and breastbone.)
2 tbsp	soya sauce
4 tbsp	jalapeño jelly
1 tbsp	freshly squeezed lemon juice
1 tbsp	chopped garlic
2 tbsp	chopped fresh herbs (thyme, oregano, coriander)
1 tbsp	vegetable oil
	salt and freshly ground black pepper to taste

1. In a large mixing bowl, mix the soya sauce, jalapeño jelly, lemon juice, garlic, herbs, oil and seasoning.

2. Marinate the hens for 4 to 6 hours, covered, in the refrigerator.

3. On a lightly greased grill over medium-high heat, barbecue the hens for 8 to 10 minutes per side, until done.

SERVES 2 TO 4.

CHICKEN BARBECUE STYLE

4	5 oz boneless chicken breasts, skin on, (trim the wing bone of all meat so that the breasts will be perfect for presentation
	salt and pepper to taste
1 tbsp	extra virgin olive oil
1 cup	gourmet barbecue sauce (use your favorite)

1. Season chicken breasts with salt, pepper and olive oil.

2. Place breasts skin-side down, on medium high heat grill for 5-6 minutes. Turn and grill 5-6 minutes on other side until the meat is firm.

3. Baste with your favorite barbecue sauce and cook for 2 more minutes each side until the sauce is caramelized.

NOTE:
Do not put the barbecue sauce on the chicken too early. The sauce is high in sugar and will burn before the chicken is fully cooked.

SERVES 4.

RAY'S CURRIED CHICKEN

This was a request from a viewer named Ray, so we named it after him.

This is a spicy curry, but you can tone it down with more yogurt.

1 tbsp	chopped garlic
1/4 cup	finely chopped onion
1 tbsp	chopped ginger
2 tbsp	lemon juice
2 tbsp	orange juice
2 tbsp	curry powder
1 1/2 tsp	chopped cilantro
1 tbsp	canola oil
1/2 cup	yogurt
6	boneless skinless chicken breasts

1. In a large bowl stir together the garlic, onion, ginger, lemon juice, orange juice, curry, cilantro, oil and yogurt.

2. With a sharp paring knife make 3-1/2-inch deep diagonal cuts in each chicken breast, being careful not to cut all the way through.

3. Rub the marinade into the chicken making sure that you get into the cuts. Pour remaining marinade on the chicken and marinate overnight covered in the refrigerator.

4. Grill the chicken on a well seasoned grill for 6 to 7 minutes per side until done.

Serve with Coconut Rice (page 108) and Grilled Vegetables.

Serves 6.

VANILLA RUM MARINATED MUSCOVY DUCK BREASTS

A Muscovy duck breast is a large duck breast. You can use wild duck breasts. The key to this dish is not to over cook the duck. Serve it medium rare so that it's tender and delicious. Quackilicious!

2 large	Muscovy duck breasts, boneless (approx. 8-10 oz each)
1 tbsp	chopped garlic
2 tbsp	pure vanilla extract
2 tbsp	chopped fresh sage
1 tbsp	cracked black pepper
2 oz	dark rum

1. Diamond-score the skin of each duck breast.

2. Mix together the garlic, vanilla, sage, black pepper and rum.

3. Rub marinade mixture all over the duck breasts, pushing the marinade into the flesh. Let marinate for 4-6 hours.

4. On a seasoned grill over medium high heat, grill the duck breasts. Start with the skin-side down. Grill for about 2-3 minutes, until the skin gets crispy.

5. Turn breasts over to meat-side down and reduce the heat to low. Close barbecue cover and continue to cook for 8 minutes for medium-rare doneness, longer for closer to well done.

6. Slice each breast thinly into 12 slices. Serve with grilled new potatoes, creme fraiche and caviar.

SERVES 4.

RASPBERRY CHICKEN

I LOVE RASPBERRIES AND I LOVE CHICKEN. THERE'S NOTHING I LIKE BETTER THAN
GOING UP TO THE COTTAGE AND PICKING WILD RASPBERRIES.
GO ON A FAMILY BERRY-HUNT, OR GO TO THE STORE, AND ADD A BIT OF FRUITINESS
TO YOUR BARBECUED CHICKEN.

6	boneless chicken breasts, with skin on

Marinade:

1/4 cup	red wine vinegar
1/4 cup	olive oil
2 tbsp	chopped fresh garlic
1 tbsp	chopped fresh thyme
1 pint	fresh raspberries squished (wild ones are best)
3/4 cup	jalapeño jelly
2 tbsp	fresh lemon juice

1. Mix the marinade ingredients together.

2. Marinate the chicken breasts for 4 to 6 hours in the marinade.

3. Prepare a baste by mixing the jalapeño jelly and the lemon juice. Barbecue
   the marinaded chicken breasts over medium-high heat for 12 to 15 minutes
   until done. While barbequing, baste with the jalapeño-lemon juice mixture.

Serve with Cambazola Cheese Polenta (page 109).

SERVES 4 TO 6.

SPIT-ROASTED SAVORY CHICKEN

THE SPIT IS ONE OF THE LEAST-USED ACCESSORIES ON A BARBECUE. BUT WHEN DONE RIGHT, THIS IS ONE SUCCULENT, DELICIOUS, OUTSTANDING CHICKEN. CHEDDAR CORN MASHED POTATOES (PAGE 111) MAKE A NICE ACCOMPANIMENT TO THIS DISH.

1	whole fresh chicken (5-8 lb)
1/4 cup	vegetable oil
3 tbsp	chopped garlic
2 tbsp	chopped fresh tarragon
1 tbsp	freshly ground black pepper
1/4 cup	sherry
	salt to taste
	barbecue seasoning to taste

1. Mix all ingredients, excluding the chicken, together and use as a baste.

2. Fasten trussed chicken to spit. The spit should enter through the backbone about 1 inch above the tail and come out through the front end of the breast bone.

3. Fasten spit to the barbecue.

4. Roast over medium heat, basting every 10-15 minutes. Cook until tender and the outside is crispy and golden. Cooking time will vary per size of the chicken. For a 5-lb bird cook for 1 1/2 to 2 hours. Test by placing a meat thermometer in the thickest part of the thigh. Temperature should be a minimum of 160°F.

SERVES 4 TO 6.

SEAFOOD

BARBECUE LOBSTER TAILS

THERE'S NOTHING BETTER THAN FRESH ATLANTIC LOBSTERS.

LOBSTER TAILS ARE DELICIOUS WHEN THEY'RE GRILLED ON THE BARBECUE;

THEY'RE TENDER AND RICH IN FLAVOR.

4	lobster tails, cut in half lengthwise
2 tbsp	lemon juice
1 tbsp	chopped fresh dill
1 tbsp	chopped fresh shallot
1 tsp	freshly ground black pepper
1 tbsp	olive oil
1/4 cup	Dijon mustard
2 tbsp	jalapeño jelly

1. In a medium bowl, mix together the lemon juice, dill, shallot, pepper, olive oil, Dijon mustard, and jalapeño jelly.

2. On a lightly greased grill over medium-heat, barbecue the lobster tail halves for 6 to 8 minutes, basting frequently with the mustard-dill basting sauce.

Serve the lobster tails with barbecue corn on the cob, and basmati rice.

SERVES 4.

BBQ GRILLED SHRIMP WITH MAPLE BEER BBQ SAUCE

2 lbs	large shrimp, peeled and deveined (about 24-30)
2 tsp	dry BBQ seasoning
1/8 cup	olive oil
1 cup	hickory BBQ sauce
1/2 cup	maple syrup
1/2 cup	beer (stout)
1 tbsp	garlic
1 tbsp	green onion
2 tbsp	lemon juice
1 tbsp	dill

1. Mix together the olive oil, hickory BBQ sauce, maple syrup, beer, garlic, green onion, lemon juice and dill.

2. Season shrimp with dry BBQ seasoning. Toss with BBQ sauce.

3. Skewer shrimp onto water-soaked bamboo skewers then grill over medium-high heat for 3-5 minutes until the shrimp are opaque and firm to the touch.

4. Remember to baste with extra sauce.

SERVES 8.

LOBSTER BOIL

═══════════

BOIL 'EM UP BIG TIME. YOU WILL NEED A VERY LARGE POT AND A
ROCKET OR PROPANE BURNER. YOU'RE GOING TO NEED LOTS OF NAPKINS
FOR THIS REAL HANDS-ON DINNER.

═══════════

8	12 oz bottles of beer
4-6 heads	garlic, halved
3	onions, quartered
2 cups	diced celery
1 bunch	green onions
1 cup	Old Bay Seasoning or Crab Boil Seasoning
1/4 cup	black peppercorns
3	lemons, halved
24-36	new mini potatoes
12 cobs	corn
12	lobsters, PEI or Atlantic
2 large bunches	asparagus

1. Fill a very large pot 1/3 full with cold water and bring to a rolling boil.

2. Add beer, garlic, onions, celery, green onions, seasoning, black peppercorns, and lemons; return to a boil.

3. Add potatoes and cook for 5 minutes.

4. Add corn and lobsters. Cover and bring back to a boil. Let cook for 10 minutes.

5. Add asparagus. Cover and cook for 2-3 minutes longer.

SERVES 12.

OVEN-ROASTED MUSSELS AND CLAMS ON THE BARBECUE

The first time I had cast-iron mussels was at a restaurant called Lulu's in San Francisco. They were crusted with sea salt and were the tastiest mussels that I've ever eaten. This is my version, done on the barbecue with some clams.

2 lbs	fresh mussels
2 lbs	fresh clams
1/2 cup	clarified butter
3 tbsp	pesto (page 25)
	sea salt

1. Preheat barbecue to high heat for 5 minutes.

2. Place a large cast-iron pan on the barbecue.

3. Close the lid. Let the pan get very hot (5 minutes). Sprinkle with sea salt.

4. Place the mussels and clams in the pan.

5. Close the lid on the barbecue. Let the shellfish cook for 5-7 minutes.

6. Check to see if the shells have opened; if so, remove the cast-iron pan from grill.

7. Mix the clarified butter and pesto together, then toss with shrimp. Serve.

Serves 8 to 10.

PICKEREL AND SCALLOP SEVICHE

A TASTE OF THE GREAT OUTDOORS. I COOKED PICKEREL WHEN I WORKED AT ROGERSON LODGES IN PORT LORING, ONTARIO. I 'D GO FISHING AND CATCH PICKEREL, SKIN AND BONE THEM, AND MAKE SEVICHE. A SEVICHE IS RAW MARINATED FISH, BUT THE MARINADE ACTUALLY COOKS THE FISH.

1/2 lb	large fresh sea scallops, sliced in half
1 lb	fresh pickerel fillets, skin and bones removed
1/4 cup	fresh lime juice
1/4 cup	fresh lemon juice
1/4 cup	chopped fresh shallot

1 tbsp	chopped fresh jalapeño
3 tbsp	chopped fresh dill or cilantro
1 tsp	chopped fresh garlic
2 tbsp	olive oil
1/2 cup	chopped fresh tomato, peeled and seeded
1 tbsp	freshly ground black pepper
1/4 cup	chopped green onion
	salt to taste

1. Slice the pickerel fillets in 1/2 inch thick strips.

2. Mix the scallops and pickerel together in large bowl.

3. Add the remaining ingredients, toss together gently. Season and cover. Let marinate for 4 to 6 hours in the refrigerator.

Serve with Louisiana Corn (page 119)

SERVES 4 TO 6.

SHRIMP AND SCALLOP SKEWERS WITH CORIANDER PESTO

18	large jumbo sea scallops, fresh or frozen
24	large jumbo shrimp, fresh or frozen (thaw seafood first if using frozen.)
6	9-inch skewers

Marinade:

1 cup	tangerine juice
1/4 cup	olive oil
1/4 cup	coriander pesto (page 139)
2 cloves	chopped fresh garlic
	freshly ground pepper to taste

1. Put scallops and shrimp on the skewers— 4 shrimp and 3 scallops per skewer

2. Mix marinade ingredients together. Marinate skewered shrimp and scallops for 2 hours in the marinade.

3. Place skewers on hot grill and barbeque for 5-6 minutes turning once.

SERVES 6.

SIDE DISHES

COCONUT RICE

SERVE THIS WITH THE CURRIED CHICKEN ON PAGE 91.

1/2 tbsp	canola oil
1 tbsp	chopped garlic
2 tsp	chopped fresh ginger
2 cups	long grain rice
3/4 cups	coconut milk
1 tsp	salt
1 tsp	chopped fresh mint

1. Heat oil in a heavy saucepan over medium heat.

2. Add garlic and ginger and cook, stirring until transparent.

3. Add rice, and stir until fully coated.

4. Add coconut milk, salt and 2 1/2 cups of water. Bring to a boil. Reduce heat to low, cover and simmer until all of the liquid is absorbed and the grains are tender, about 18 to 20 minutes.

5. Remove pan from heat and let stand, covered, for 5 minutes. Add mint and serve.

SERVES 6.

CAMBAZOLA CHEESE POLENTA

4 cups	water
1 tsp	salt
1 1/2 cups	polenta, corn meal
2	green onions, diced
4 oz	Cambazola cheese, diced
2 oz	Parmesan cheese
2 tbsp	butter
	salt and pepper to taste
1/4 cup	chopped basil for garnish

1. Place the water and salt in a heavy pot, bring to boil, then slowly add the polenta, stirring constantly. Reduce heat to low and while continuing to stir, cook for 15-20 minutes until the polenta is creamy.

2. Add the green onions, cheese and butter, stir until the cheese melts and all is incorporated. Adjust seasoning and garnish with chopped basil. Serve with Raspberry Chicken on page 94.

SERVES 4.

RISOTTO LIME AND ROASTED PEPPER

SERVE THIS WITH THE SHRIMP AND SCALLOP SKEWERS ON PAGE 105.

2 tbsp	butter
2 tbsp	chopped fresh shallots
1 1/2 cups	arborio rice
1/4 cup	white wine

5 cups	fish or vegetable stock
1	large roasted green pepper, peeled, seeded and diced 1/4 inch
1 tbsp	chopped fresh lemon thyme
1/4 cup	fresh lime juice
1/4 cup	fresh grated Regianno Parmesan cheese

1. In a medium-sized saucepan over medium heat, place the butter and shallots.

2. Sauté the shallots for 2 minutes until transparent.

3. Add the rice and stir making sure to coat the rice with butter mixture.

4. Add white wine and stir for 2 to 3 minutes or until the rice has absorbed the wine.

5. Now add the stock in 3 equal parts stirring constantly. When the rice has absorbed the first amount of stock then add the next part and so on.

6. When the rice is done, approximately 20 minutes, add the remaining ingredients, and serve.

SERVES 4 TO 6.

SWEET POTATO ROSTI (PANCAKE)

1 lb	sweet potatoes, blanched until just cooked, chilled and grated
1	large egg
1/2 cup	grated cooking onion
1 tbsp	chopped rosemary
2 tbsp	olive oil
2 tbsp	butter
	salt and pepper to taste

1. Mix all ingredients together.

2. In a medium-sized non-stick fry pan over medium-high heat, fry half of the mixture in 1 tbsp of oil and 1 tbsp of butter.

3. Fry for 3 to 5 minutes per side, until golden brown and crispy.

4. Repeat with other half so you have two pancakes.

5. Slice in half and serve with Black Bean Quail (page 88) and fresh baby greens.

SERVES 4

CHEDDAR CORN MASHED POTATOES

2 lb	Yukon Gold potatoes, peeled
1/4 cup	spiced olive oil
1/4 cup	unsalted butter
3 to 4	ears of corn
1 tbsp	chopped garlic
1/4 cup	chopped green onion
1 1/2 cup	old cheddar cheese, grated
	salt and pepper to taste

1. Place the potatoes in a saucepan and cover with cold water by about 2-3 inches. Bring the water to a boil, then reduce heat to medium-low (a simmer). Cook the potatoes for approximately 35-45 minutes, until they are tender.

2. Drain the potatoes and return to heat. Shake pan well until excess moisture evaporates, about 1 minute. Potatoes should be dry to the touch.

3. Mash the potatoes, add the remaining ingredients, stirring to incorporate evenly. Season and serve.

SERVES 6.

VEGETABLES

BAKED POTATOES

large baking potatoes (1 per person)
olive oil
salt and pepper
barbecue seasoning (any commercial spice blend will do)

1. Pre-heat an oven to 400°F.

2. Wash potatoes under cold water to remove all traces of soil. Dry with paper towel and prick in several places with a fork.

3. Place the potatoes in the oven on a center rack and bake until tender and soft (about 1 hour).

4. Remove from oven and cut in half lengthwise. Season with salt, pepper, barbecue seasoning and oil.

5. Barbecue over medium high heat flat-side down to start for about 3 minutes per side until slightly crispy.

6. Serve with butter, sour cream and fresh chives.

GRILLED PORTOBELLO MUSHROOMS

6 to 8	medium-size portobello mushrooms
1/2 cup	balsamic vinegar
3 tbsp	chopped fresh coriander
1 tbsp	coarsely ground pepper
1 tsp	finely chopped garlic
1 tsp	salt
1 cup	roasted garlic-flavored olive oil

1. Clean mushrooms with soft brush or damp cloth. Remove stems— reserve for other use.

2. Prepare marinade: Mix together vinegar, coriander, pepper, garlic and salt. Gradually whisk in oil until mixture is thickened.

3. Brush mushrooms all over with marinade, reserving extra marinade to use as a basting sauce. Arrange mushrooms gill-side up in shallow dish, cover loosely and let marinate in refrigerator for 4 to 6 hours.

4. Place in grill basket or directly on grill over medium-high heat and cook 8 to 10 minutes per side or until tender, basting frequently with reserves marinade.

5. Slice mushrooms but do not separate slices. Arrange on large platter.

SERVES 6 TO 8.

GRILLED ASPARAGUS

1 bunch	fresh asparagus (large bunch 1 1/2 lb.)
2 tbsp	olive oil
1/4 cup	raspberry vinegar

1. Break or cut ends off spears. Marinate asparagus in mixture of oil and vinegar for 2 to 3 hours.

2. Arrange asparagus on a plate and cover with plastic wrap.

3. Microwave at high for 1 minute.

4. Place directly on grill or in a grill basket over medium-high heat and cook for 8 to 10 minutes or until tender and lightly charred, turning periodically.

SERVES 4.

COTTAGE COUNTRY BAKED BEANS

When working at Rogerson's Lodges in 1984, I made these delicious baked beans every Friday for our Pickerel Fish Fry.

6 slices	bacon, diced
1	large onion, diced
1 tbsp	chopped garlic
2 stalks	celery diced
1/4 cup	molasses
1/4 cup	ketchup
1 tsp	mustard powder
4 cups	navy beans, canned or cooked dry beans
	salt, pepper, hot sauce and worcestershire to taste
1 10 oz can	plum tomatoes, drained and diced

1. In a medium fry pan, fry the bacon until just crisp, add onion, garlic and celery and continue to cook for 5 minutes stirring occasionally.

2. Remove from pan and place into a large oven-proof baking dish.

3. Add molasses, ketchup, mustard, beans and diced tomato. Season with salt, pepper, hot sauce and worcestershire to taste.

4. Cover and place in a preheated 375 degree F. oven and bake for 40 minutes.

Serves 8 to 10.

GRILLED SUMMER ZUCCHINI

2	medium green zucchini
1	medium yellow zucchini
1	medium marrow
3 tbsp	vegetable oil
1 tbsp	red wine vinegar
1 tsp	freshly ground black pepper

1. Slice the zucchini and marrow lengthwise into four equal portions. Toss in vegetable oil, pepper and vinegar until evenly coated.

2. Grill over medium high heat, turning once, until tender and slightly charred.

Serve with the Stuffed Pork Chops (page 76).

SERVES 6 TO 8.

GRILLED SWEET POTATOES

4 tbsp	Dijon mustard
1/2 cup	maple syrup
2 tsp	lemon juice
5	sweet potatoes, cooked until tender but still a bit firm
1/4 cup	olive oil
	salt and pepper to taste

1. In a bowl mix together the mustard, maple syrup, lemon juice, salt and pepper.

2. Slice potatoes into 1/4-inch thick rounds and toss with olive oil, salt and pepper.

3. Grill over medium-high heat for about 3 to 4 minutes per side until slightly charred and crispy. Add to mustard, maple syrup mix, season and serve.

SERVES 4.

LOUISIANA CORN

3 tbsp	vegetable oil
2 tbsp	unsalted butter
1 cup	finely chopped onion
1 1/2 cups	chopped fresh tomato (peeled and seeded)
1 cup	chopped roasted red pepper
1 tbsp	garlic
2 tbsp	chopped fresh chili
1/4 cup	chopped green onion
2 cups	sugar snap peas
6 ears	fresh corn or 2 cups of thawed frozen kernels
2 tbsp	white wine tarragon vinegar

1. If using fresh corn, cut the kernels off the cob.

2. In a large frypan, melt the oil and butter, add the onion, garlic and chili and sauté for 2 minutes until tender.

3. Add the snap peas, tomato, pepper, green onion and corn and cook for 5 minutes, stirring occasionally. Adjust seasoning and serve.

SERVES 6 TO 8.

HOW TO
ROAST PEPPERS

1. Leave peppers whole, or cut in half and remove seeds and ribs.

2. Place on the rack in a pre-heated oven at 450°F. Cook for 10 to 15 minutes until peppers become black and blistered.

3. Remove from oven, immediately place peppers in a plastic bag and seal it tight.

    Allow peppers to cool 10 minutes.

4. Remove peppers from the bag and the skin will peel off with ease.

LIFETIME IS 3 DAYS.

SUGAR SNAP PEAS
AND BEANS

2 tbsp	extra virgin olive oil
2 cups	fresh sugar snap peas
1 cup	fresh green beans
1 cup	fresh yellow beans
3 tbsp	balsamic vinegar
	salt and pepper to taste

1. Over medium-high heat in a sauté pan, preheat the olive oil for 30 seconds.

2. Add sugar snap peas and the beans. Sauté for 1-2 minutes.

3. Add seasoning and balsamic vinegar. Toss and serve.

SERVES 4.

VANILLA PARSNIPS

4-6	large parsnips, peeled, ends and tips removed
1	vanilla bean, split down the middle
	vegetable oil for brushing
	salt and pepper to taste

1. Bring pot of water to a boil.

2. Place parsnips and vanilla bean in water. Blanch for 5-7 minutes.

3. Remove from pot, let cool on a tray.

4. Discard water and vanilla bean.

5. Slice parsnips in half. Brush with some vegetable oil.

6. Season with salt and pepper

7. Grill the parsnips on medium high heat for 12 -15 minutes, turning once.

SERVES 4 TO 6.

VEGETABLES PROVENÇAL

2 each	green and yellow zucchini, sliced crossways into 1/2-inch rounds
1	red onion, cut into 1-inch dice
1 pint	cherry tomatoes, cut in halves
1/4 cup	chopped garlic in oil
1/4 cup	chopped fresh tarragon
1/4 cup	fresh sage
1/2 cup	butter

1. Place all the ingredients in a large bowl and gently combine, using a wooden spoon or your hands.

2. Make a large pouch with aluminum foil. Place vegetable mixture in the foil pouch and enclose by folding the edges over.

3. Heat on high on grill for 15 minutes.

4. Remove foil pouch from grill; let stand for 2 minutes.

5. Open foil pouch carefully. Transfer vegetables to a bowl; season with salt and fresh cracked black pepper.

SERVES 4 TO 6.

BALSAMIC GRILLED RED ONIONS

1	large red onion sliced into 3/4" thick rounds
1/8 cup	balsamic vinegar
1 tbsp	olive oil
	salt and pepper to taste

1. Mix together red onion rings, vinegar, olive oil, and seasonings.

2. Barbecue on a lightly greased grill over medium-high heat for 3 to 5 minutes, until lightly charred and tender.

SERVES 4.

GRILLED NEW POTATOES FOR COWBOY STEAK

1 lb	small, new potatoes
2 tbsp	butter
2 tbsp	chopped fresh dill
1 tbsp	freshly squeezed lemon juice
	salt and freshly ground black pepper to taste

1. Blanch new potatoes in boiling water for 10-12 minutes or until tender.

2. Place potatoes in a barbecue basket and grill over medium-high for 8-10 minutes until golden brown.

3. Remove the potatoes from the basket and in a medium-sized bowl, toss the potatoes with butter, dill, lemon juice and seasoning.

SERVES 4.

SANDWICHES

MUFFULETTA

My version of this famous sandwich. I love a great sandwich and whenever I am in New Orleans, it is a must that I have this awesome sandwich. Minimum a half will do with an ice cold beer.

1 cup	diced pitted green olives
1/2 cup	diced sundried tomato
1/2 cup	chopped roasted red peppers
1/2 cup	diced red onion
3 filets	anchovy, mashed
1 tsp	chopped garlic
2 tsp	chopped Italian parsley
1 tsp	oregano, diced
1/2 tsp	black pepper
1 tbsp	balsamic vinegar
1/4 cup	olive oil
1 round	Italian sesame loaf (8" in diameter)
2 cups	arugula
1 large	tomato, thinly sliced
4 oz, each	mortadella, spicy Italian salami and sweet capicollo, all thinly sliced
4 oz	provolone cheese, thinly sliced
2 oz	asiago cheese, grated

1. In a bowl, mix together the olives, sundried tomato, red pepper, onion, anchovy, garlic, parsley, oregano, pepper, vinegar and oil; cover and refrigerate for 4-6 hours or overnight.

2. Cut the bread horizontally, taking the top off of the loaf, remove the soft bread dough leaving a bowl-like loaf.

3. Drain the olive salad and brush the inside of the loaf and the top outside cover. Fill with the olive salad and pack down evenly.

4. Add the arugula, tomato slices, mortadella, salami, capicollo and cheeses, in layers; top with bread cover.

5. Wrap tightly in plastic wrap and refrigerate for 1 hour. Slice and serve.

Serves 6.

SUPER BURGERS

When making beef or lamb burgers, you need a meat mixture of 25% fat to meat, and you need to season the meat. Shaping the burger is also important—try to make them a uniform size. Use only fresh ground beef or lamb.

Beef Burgers

1 lb	medium ground beef
4 oz	extra old cheddar
	barbecue spice seasoning mix

Lamb Burgers

1 lb	medium ground lamb
4 oz	blue cheese
	barbecue spice seasoning mix

1. Pre-heat the barbecue to 500°F or high heat. Form the meat into patties. 1 lb of meat will make 2 8-oz burgers.

2. Place the burgers on the barbecue and cook for 3-5 minutes per side for a medium rare burger.

3. Season both sides of the burgers with your favorite barbecue spice seasoning mix.

4. Place cheese (2 oz per burger) on each burger, close the lid of the barbecue and melt the cheese for 1 minute.

5. Toast your favorite hamburger buns and use your favorite condiments for super beef and lamb burgers.

Serves 4.

MONSTER TURKEY BURGERS

2 lbs	lean ground turkey
1/3 cup	seasoned breadcrumbs
3 tbsp	fresh lemon juice
2 tsp	fresh chopped sage
1	medium red onion, finely chopped, sautéed until caramelized
1 cup	grated Swiss cheese

| 1 tbsp | olive oil |
| | salt and freshly ground pepper to taste |

1. Preheat grill to medium high.

2. Combine all ingredients in a large bowl and mix thoroughly.

3. Divide mixture and form into 6 equal patties.

4. Grill patties for about 5-6 minutes per side.

5. Serve with a fresh berry relish as is, or on a bun.

SERVES 6.

GRILLED SWORDFISH AND WATERCRESS PANINI

SWORDFISH IS A MEATY FISH—STEAK OF THE SEA. YOU COULD ALSO USE TUNA, MARLIN OR SHARK.

2 slices	fresh swordfish steaks (but some frozen products are excellent) about 1/2" thick, 4-6 oz each
2 tbsp	extra virgin olive oil
2 tbsp	chopped fresh herbs (a blend of chive, parsley, thyme and basil is wonderful)
	salt and freshly ground pepper to taste
4 slices	fresh Italian or home-style bread
1/2 bunch	watercress, cleaned and thick stems removed
4 slices	fresh ripe tomato

1. Moisten the swordfish on both sides with 1 tbsp of olive oil. Grill the swordfish over medium heat for 3 minutes per side.

2. Coat with the chopped fresh herb and season to taste. Cook for an additional 30 seconds to 1 minute per side.

3. Brush the bread with 1 tbsp of olive oil and, as the fish is finishing, grill it until golden brown.

4. Place the watercress on the bottom slice of bread. Top with the tomato slices (grill them if you want) and swordfish. Top with the Onion Caper Salsa (page 142) and the final slice of bread.

SERVES 2.

SOFT SHELL CRAB SANDWICH

═══════════

I HAD MY FIRST SOFT SHELL CRAB IN CRISFIELF, MARYLAND
ON CHESAPEAKE BAY. IT WAS SERVED ON A KAISER ROLL WITH TARTAR SAUCE
AND ICEBERG LETTUCE. WHAT A SANDWICH!

═══════════

3	jumbo soft shell crabs, dressed
3	Italian loaves
	olive oil for brushing
	balsamic vinegar for brushing

Marinade:

1/4 cup	olive oil
1/4 cup	tequila
1/4 cup	lime juice
1/8 cup	chopped garlic
2 tbsp	chopped coriander
1 tbsp	cracked black pepper

1. Blend the marinade ingredients together. Marinate crabs for 2 to 4 hours.

2. Barbecue over medium-high heat for 4 to 5 minutes per side until crispy.

3. Cut the Italian loaves in half, grill, then brush with olive oil and (balsamic vinegar. Place the grilled crab on the bread. Garnish with baby greens, tartar sauce and field fresh tomatoes.

SERVES 4 TO 6.

VEGETABLE BURRITOS

A ROLLED-UP SANDWICH.

1 1/2 cups	shredded Napa cabbage
1/2 cup	mushrooms, julienne
1/4 cup	fresh chopped coriander
1 tbsp	fresh lime juice
1/2 cup	Monterey Jack cheese
1/2 cup	cheddar cheese, shredded
1/4 cup	carrots, shredded
1	jalapeño pepper, fine-julienne
	salt to season
8	11-inch flour tortillas
	spicy plum sauce
	oil

1. Combine first 9 ingredients except tortillas in a large mixing bowl; season with salt.

2. Place about 1/4 cup of filling in each tortilla and wrap as you would a spring roll.

3. When closing each tortilla, brush the end with some spicy plum sauce to act as an adhesive.

4. Preheat barbecue to medium heat.

5. Brush each burrito with some oil and place on the barbecue.

6. Grill burritos for 3-5 minutes, just to heat them through.

7. Transfer burritos to a plate. Slice into desired sizes, or serve whole, accompanied with Queso Blanco Salsa (page 141).

MAKES 8 SERVINGS.

CONDIMENTS

ROASTED GARLIC AND BALSAMIC BUTTER

1 lb	butter, salted
1/4 cup	balsamic vinegar
1 head	roasted garlic, mashed
1 tbsp	chopped fresh thyme
1 tsp	coarse ground black pepper

1. Soften butter.

2. Mix butter with vinegar, garlic, thyme and pepper.

3. Blend until incorporated.

4. Serve with grilled vegetables, breads and meats.

MAKES 1 CUP.

BANANA SALSA

1-1/2 cups	chopped fresh banana
1 whole	jalapeño pepper, seeded and diced
1/4 cup	diced red pepper
1 tbsp	chopped fresh mint
1 tbsp	chopped onion
2 tbsp	lime juice, freshly squeezed

Mix all the ingredients and let stand for 1 hour before serving, to let all the flavors come together. Serve with your favorite ice cream.

MAKES 2 CUPS.

BEER AND CHEESE FONDUE

2 cloves	garlic
1 1/2 cup	beer
1 lb.	Swiss cheese
1 lb.	cheddar cheese
1 tbsp.	cornstarch
1/4 cup	cold beer
pinch	baking soda
	fresh-ground black or white pepper

1. Place garlic and beer in a pot over low heat.

2. When beer is steaming, gradually stir in cheeses, waiting for one handful to melt before adding the next.

3. After all cheese has been added, stir and continue to cook for 5 minutes.

4. Dissolve cornstarch in cold beer, and add to melted cheese mixture.

5. Stir in baking soda until foam subsides.

6. Season with pepper.

MAKES 4 CUPS.

BOURBON AND MUSTARD MARINADE

THE BOURBON IN THIS DISH GIVES IT A SMOKY CORN AND OAK KICK.

1 1/2 cup	Bourbon whisky
1/3 cup	canola oil
1/2 cup	grainy pommery mustard
1/4 cup	Worcestershire sauce
3 tbsp	brown sugar or maple syrup
2 tbsp	chopped garlic
1 tbsp	chopped fresh sage
	freshly ground black pepper to taste

Combine all of the ingredients and whisk to emulsify.

MAKES APPROXIMATELY 3 CUPS.

CORIANDER PESTO

2 bunches	fresh coriander, wash and remove stems
1/2 cup	roasted pine nuts
1/4 cup	chopped fresh garlic
1/4 cup	olive oil
1/8 cup	lime juice
	salt and pepper to taste

In a food processor blend all ingredients together to a paste.

MAKES 1 CUP.

SMOKY CORN SALSA

1 tbsp	extra virgin olive oil
1 cup	fresh corn kernels (frozen will do)
1/2 cup	chopped onion
1 tbsp	chopped fresh garlic
1/2 cup	chopped red pepper
1 tbsp	chopped fresh coriander
1/2 cup	spicy thick and chunky commercial salsa

1. Heat a medium pan over high heat for 1 minute. Add olive oil, corn, onion, garlic and red pepper, stirring continuously over high heat for 2-3 minutes, until the corn starts to turn golden brown.

2. Add coriander and salsa. Cook for another 2 minutes. Serve with lamb chops.

MAKES 3 CUPS.

CRAZY LARRY'S BARBECUE SPICE

8 tbsp	paprika
4 tbsp	chili powder
2 tbsp	ground coriander
2 tbsp	salt
2 tbsp	sugar
1 tbsp	dry mustard
1 tbsp	black pepper
1 tbsp	dried thyme
1 tbsp	curry powder
1 tbsp	cayenne pepper

Mix all ingredients together and store in a cool, dry place.

MINTY TZATZIKI SAUCE

1 1/2 cups	plain yogurt (the thicker the better)
1 1/2 cups	English cucumber, peeled and grated, excess juice removed
2 tbsp	chopped fresh garlic
1 tsp	chopped fresh mint
pinch	sugar
2 tsp	lemon juice
	salt and freshly ground pepper to taste

1. In a medium bowl mix the yogurt, drained cucumber, garlic, mint, sugar, lemon juice and seasoning.

2. Let stand refrigerated for 1 hour.

SERVES 6 TO 8.

PEACH SALSA

8	peaches, grilled and chopped finely
1/4 cup	wine vinegar
1/2 cup	diced tomato
2 tbsp	sugar
2 tbsp	olive oil
1 tbsp	chopped mint
to taste	salt and pepper

Mix all the ingredients and serve with curried chicken.

MAKES 2 CUPS.

QUESO BLANCO SALSA

2 cups	softened cream cheese
2 oz	gold tequila
1 tbsp	finely chopped jalapeño pepper
1 tbsp	finely chopped green onions
1/2	avocado, cut into 1/2-inch cubes

Put all ingredients in a pot and melt together over low heat. Season with salt as desired.

MAKES 2 CUPS.

RASPBERRY BUTTER

1/2 lb	softened unsalted butter
1/8 tsp	salt
1 tbsp	freshly cracked black pepper
1/2 pint	fresh raspberries
squeeze of	lemon

Blend above ingredients together until the butter is a wonderful pink colour with the flavor of the raspberries throughout.

MAKES 2 CUPS.

RED ONION & CAPER SALSA

2 tbsp	chopped red onion
2 tbsp	coarsely chopped capers
1 tsp	chopped fresh dill
1 tsp	lemon juice
1 tsp	olive oil
	salt and freshly ground pepper to taste

Blend all the ingredients together.

SERVES 2.

TOMATO SALSA

2 cups	tomato, chopped
1/2 cup	red onion, chopped
1/2 cup	red pepper, diced
1/2 cup	green pepper, diced
1 tbsp	chopped fresh garlic
3 tbsp	jalapeño pepper, chopped (use less if you don't want it too spicy)
1 tbsp	freshly squeezed lime juice
1 tbsp	coriander, chopped
1 tbsp	vegetable oil
	salt and freshly ground black pepper to taste

In a medium-sized bowl, mix all ingredients together. Chill for 1 to 2 hours until the flavors have blended.

Serve with fajitas, or as a dip.

MAKES 3 1/2 CUPS.

WILD MUSHROOM SALSA

2 tbsp	bacon, fully cooked and diced
1/2 lb	assorted wild mushrooms, sliced (shiitake, oyster, cremini, field, morel)
1 tbsp	chopped fresh cilantro
1 whole	jalapeño pepper, seeded and diced
1/8 tsp	salt
1/4 cup	chopped onion
1/4 cup	chopped red pepper
2 tbsp	fresh squeezed lime juice
1 tbsp	extra virgin olive oil

In a sauté-pan over medium heat, add all the above ingredients and cook for 5 minutes until mushrooms are tender. Chill and serve.

MAKES 1 CUP.

SAGE AND PEPPER BUTTER

3 tsp	cracked peppercorns (black, pink, green or white will do)
1 cup	unsalted butter, softened
1/3 cup	dark rum
2 tbsp	chopped fresh sage
	salt to taste

1. In a medium bowl with a rubber spatula or whisk, mix the peppercorns, butter, rum, sage and salt.

2. Place in a container and refrigerate until needed.

MAKES 1 CUP.

DESSERTS
&
DRINKS

DESSERTS

I BELIEVE THAT IN THE SUMMERTIME, THE BEST DESSERT IS FRESH BERRIES WITH A PINCH OF SUGAR OR SOME ICE CREAM. A FRESH PEACH, PEAR, A CRISP AND CRUNCHY APPLE — THAT IS THE BEST DESSERT GOING.

BLUEBERRY FOOL

1 pint	fresh wild blueberries (or cultivated and frozen if you can't get wild)
1 cup	granulated sugar
4 oz	Cassis liqueur
1/2 piece	vanilla bean
2 cups	35% whipping cream
1/4 cup	chopped pecans

1. In a medium saucepan over medium-high heat, bring the blueberries, sugar, cassis and vanilla to a boil. Turn the heat to low and let simmer for 10-15 minutes, until mixture is thick.

2. Remove mixture from pan and place in a bowl in the refrigerator to chill for 2 hours.

3. While the blueberry mixture is chilling, whip the whipping cream to stiff peaks.

4. Once the blueberry mixture is chilled, fold it into the whipping cream along with the chopped pecans. Be careful not to over-mix, as this will remove air from the whipped cream.

5. Place in serving dished and garnish with fresh mint leaves

SERVES 4.

GRILLED FRUIT SALAD

WHEN YOU GRILL FRUIT, IT EXTRACTS AND WARMS THE SUGARS,

MAKING THE FRUIT EVEN SWEETER THAN IT NORMALLY IS. GRILLED PINEAPPLE

IS ONE OF MY FAVORITE GRILLED FRUITS.

1 cup	red grapes
1 cup	green grapes
1/4	honey dew melon, peeled, seeded and cubed 2 inches
1/4	cantaloupe melon, peeled, seeded and cubed 2 inches
1/2	medium pineapple, peeled and cubed 2 inches
2	small starfruit , sliced 1/4 inches thick
4	baby bananas, skinned and halved
6	figs, halved
8	large strawberries, halved
4	kiwis, peeled and halved
1	mango, peeled and sliced

1. Mix all of the fruit and place in a fine mesh barbecue basket.

2. Grill over medium-high heat for 8 to 10 minutes per side until lightly charred and golden.

Vinaigrette:

1 tbsp	ginger
2 tbsp	chopped fresh mint
1/4 cup	maple syrup
1 tsp	curry powder
1/2 cup	Champagne or sparkling wine
1/8 cup	rice vinegar
1/4 cup	freshly squeezed orange juice

1. Julienne the ginger and poach for 3 minutes in 1 cup of water and 1 tsp of sugar.

2. In a mixing bowl, whisk together the ginger, mint, curry, vinegar, orange juice, maple syrup, and champagne. Pour over the grilled fruit.

Serve over your favorite vanilla ice cream!

SERVES 6 TO 8.

DRINKS

CRANRASPBERRY FIZZ

AN EASY AND REFRESHING SUMMER DRINK!

1 pint	fresh raspberries, slightly squished
3 cups	cranberry juice
3 cups	ginger ale
2 cups	crushed ice

In a large pitcher, mix the raspberries, cranberry juice, ginger ale, and ice. Stir and serve.

SERVES 4 TO 6.

FRUIT SMOOTHY

1	large banana, peeled
8	large strawberries, trimmed
2	kiwis, peeled
12 to 16	ice cubes
2 tbsp	chopped fresh mint
2 cups	freshly squeezed orange juice

In a blender, mix the banana, strawberries, kiwis, ice cubes, mint, and orange juice. Blend until smooth, and serve.

SERVES 4 TO 6.